President Clinton's Legacy to Africa

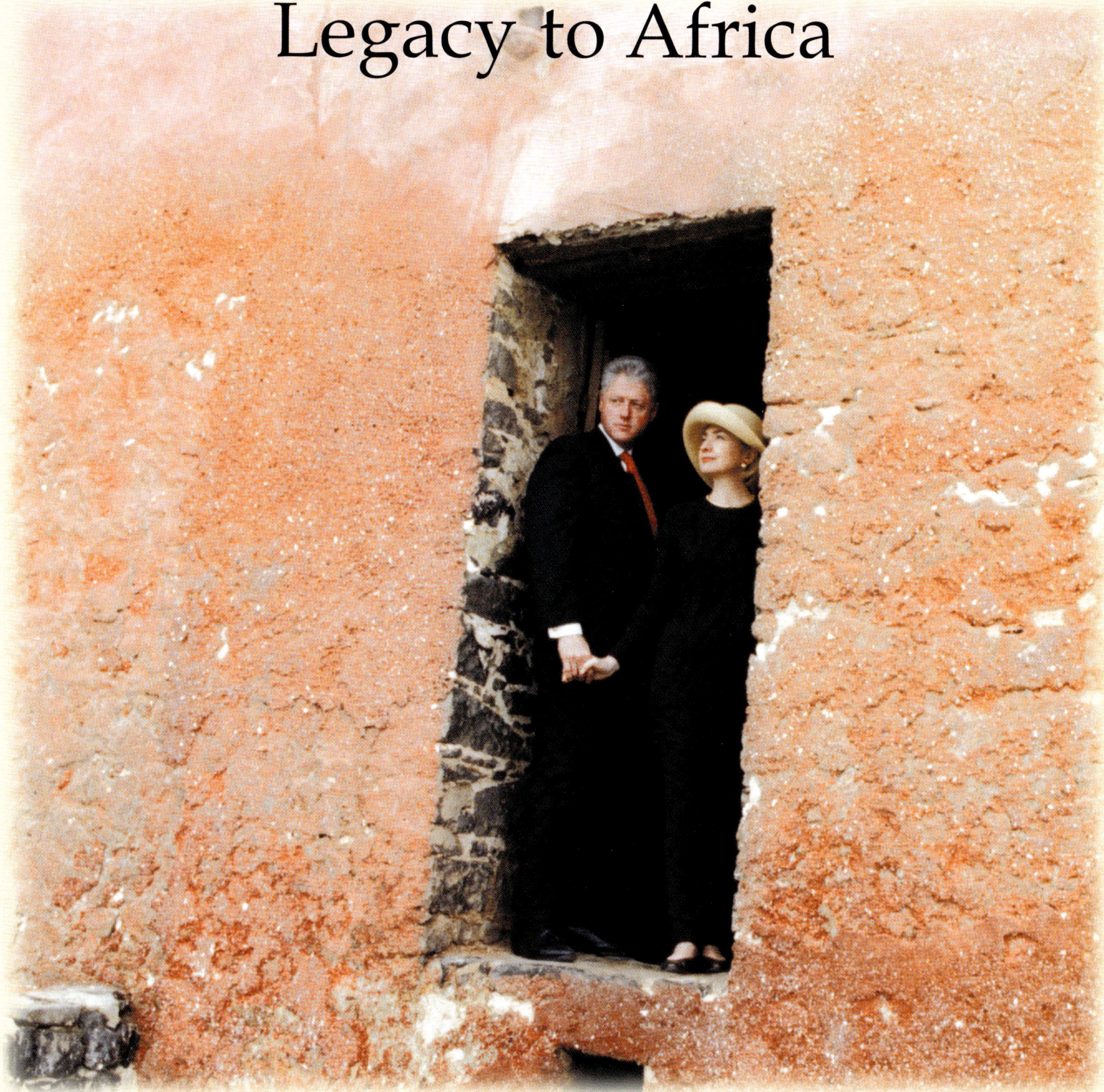

President William Jefferson Clinton and First Lady Hillary Rodham Clinton look out over the Atlantic Ocean from the infamous "door of no return" at the slave house on Goree Island in Senegal, where thousands of Africans were captured into slavery. Senegal was President Clinton's last port of call on his 1998 six-nation tour of Africa.

**AFRICAN COMMUNICATIONS AGENCY
PUBLISHING
(ACAP)**

Alhaji Bamanga Tukur, Chairman
Dr. Erieka Bennett, Vice Chairman
Samuel Dossou, Member of the Board of Directors
Dr. Khalid Abdullah Tariq Al-Mansour, Member of the Board of Directors
Charlette Neighbors, Founding Member of the Board of Directors
Dr. Babacar Ndiaye, Member of the Board of Directors
Abdul Latif Bennett, Chief Executive Officer
Anita Omitowoju, Consultant
Victoria Ogun, Marketing Director
Yemi Etta, Project Manager/Research Associate
Tony Regusters, Video Producer/Interviewer

The Legacy is the first in a series of books that the African Communications Agency Publishing (ACAP) will publish. Our goal is to continue to create a positive image of Africa in America and around the world.

To order copies of **The Legacy**, please call 866/225-ACAP, visit our web site www.acapublishing.com, or write P.O Box 39281, Washington, D.C. 20016

Copyright © 2001 by ACAP
First Edition January 2001
ISBN 0-9707202-0-3

Printed in the United States of America

President Clinton's
Trips to Africa

March 23–April 2, 1998
South Africa
Senegal
Botswana
Uganda
Ghana
Rwanda

August 25–29, 2000
Nigeria
Tanzania
Egypt

Senegal

Ghana

Nigeria

Uganda

Rwanda

Tanzania

Botswana

South Africa

Table of Contents

President William Jefferson Clinton and then President Nelson Mandela during the arrival ceremony in Cape Town, South Africa.

*Intro*duction

by Alhaji Bamanga Tukur and Dr. Erieka Bennett

Alhaji Bamanga Tukur, Chairman of ACA

Dr. Erieka Bennett, Vice Chair of ACA

The Legacy is an account of how the leader of the free world has used the politics of inclusion, mutual respect, partnership, and genuine interest to improve U.S. relations with the entire continent of Africa. Not only are current U.S.-Africa programs and policies mutually beneficial, they are often Africa-led and inclusive of Africans at every level of decision-making. This fact alone is a historic leap in U.S.-Africa relations. Early on, President Clinton admitted America's past indifference and, often, neglect of Africa. But he never allowed excuses to stop progress. In fact, this book illustrates how President Clinton forged ahead to build equal partnerships.

When one looks at the picture of President Clinton holding a newborn African infant as if he were the proud parent, one cannot help but be touched by his humanity. And he has demonstrated this humanity time and again. He responded to flood-ravaged Mozambique, he appropriated money for AIDs prevention, and he had no qualms about supporting the presence of peacekeepers to deal with centuries-old conflicts.

When you see the photograph of President Clinton in Nigeria, comfortably wearing traditional native clothing, you can see that he feels at home and was welcomed like a brother returning from the seas. In Nigeria, he was given a traditional name that means, "The son has returned home."

One cannot view the picture of President and Mrs. Clinton at the "Door of No Return" on Goree Island and not feel the heaviness that weighed on the first couple, who later remarked how poignant it was to return to that hallowed place with the descendants of slaves who were now cabinet members and lawmakers.

We wrote this book to reveal a side of the American Presidency you may never see again. By drawing attention to it, however, we pray the new administration will continue this legacy.

For three years the African Communications Agency has attempted to showcase Africa in a positive light. ACA has shared countless collaborations with the African Business Roundtable and multinational corporations in an effort to build understanding of and respect for Africa.

This book illustrates how President Clinton practiced what he preached at home before he ventured abroad to sell democracy, peace, economic development, and even trade. He embraced America's rich diversity and called attention to the need for racial healing and reconciliation in America. As he met Africans, President Clinton proudly stated that he appointed the most diverse Cabinet and administration in the nation's history. African Americans comprise 12 percent of the Cabinet and 14 percent of the political appointees, twice as many as in any previous Administration.

Many Africans recognized and appreciated the significance of President Clinton appointing the Reverend Jesse Jackson as Presidential Special Envoy to Africa and Rosa Whitaker, the first Assistant U.S. Trade Representative to Africa.

President Clinton also made the first trip by a sitting U.S. president to Ghana, Uganda, South Africa, Botswana, Rwanda, and Senegal in 1998, and he returned in 2000 to travel to Nigeria and Tanzania. These visits were not devoid of purpose and full of empty promises. President Clinton focused on key issues of development, trade, investment, education, democracy, the empowerment of women, energy, and the environment. The trips increased and enhanced ties with Africa and built on the hard work and achievements of the late Commerce Secretary Ron Brown.

The Legacy is the first in a series of books the African Communications Agency will publish. Our goal is to continue to create a positive image of Africa in the United States and around the world. We appreciate President Clinton's dedication and look forward to America's continued commitment to visionary U.S.-Africa policies.

As founders of the African Communications Agency, we envision Africans and Americans working together and forging alliances to ensure that Africa takes its rightful place in society as the cradle of civilization. This book is the beginning of this vision — Americans and Africans coming together to record this new chapter in U.S.-Africa relations.

President Olusegun Obasanjo of Nigeria greets President Clinton on his arrival at Nnamdi Azikiwe International Airport Abuja. President Obasanjo is the first Nigerian to have hosted two U.S. Presidents. As military Head of State in 1978, he received President Jimmy Carter in Lagos.

Promoting Peace and Democracy

If we wish to deepen peace and prosperity and democracy for ourselves, we must wish it also for the people of Africa. Africa is the cradle of humanity, but also a big part of humanity's future.

President William Jefferson Clinton
National Summit on Africa
February 17, 2000

The genesis of President William Jefferson Clinton's legacy to Africa is his 21st century vision of peace and democracy for the people of Africa. Consistently referring to Africa as "the cradle of humanity," he recognized early on that while the continent is blessed with a plethora of natural resources its most precious resource is the 739 million men, women, and children who live on Earth's second largest continent.

Historically, America had been preoccupied with African poverty, famine, genocide, and other negative aspects. President Clinton saw beyond Africa's problems and challenges to explore its enormous opportunities, to envision the promise of this vast land and diverse peoples, and to expand partnerships for peace and democracy that would in turn improve the lives of Africans politically, economically, and socially. He forged bridges that extended beyond African aid to the continent of Africa as an "equal partner" in the global community.

Seeking to look beyond the narrow realm of the political world, President Clinton focused on the much broader picture of a partnership with a vibrant, growing Africa that is democratic, respects human rights, and prospers economically. And, most important, to help every African "do better, to reach higher, and to fulfill dreams" as he so aptly stated during the U.S.-Africa Ministerial Conference.

Before 1990, only four Sub-Saharan countries were democracies, according to the U.S. State Department. Today, nearly half of Africa's 48 countries have instituted democratic forms of government. Therefore, the "African Renaissance," as first noted by South African President Thabo Mbeki, is currently political, social, and economic.

There are no perfect democracies and Americans personally experienced this reality during the 2000 presidential elections. For more than 224 years, America has been learning and often discovering new meanings and ideals its forefathers never imagined.

In Uganda, local government elections were completed in April 1998, following President Clinton's visit, signaling completion of the country's return to democratically elected civilian rule. One third of those newly elected officials – 11,000 — are women, as mandated by the Constitution. First Lady Hillary Rodham Clinton, in her speech at Makerere University, announced that the U.S. government would provide $2 million to help train female elected local government officials.

Ultimately, building stronger communities and a more stable society is what can be accomplished by people who have the means to freely choose their leaders, publish their thoughts, organize their labor, and invest their capital. Numerous countries including South Africa, Nigeria, Senegal, Ghana, Mali, Gabon, Uganda, and Botswana have embraced democracy.

✤

Dr. Babacar Ndiaye, Ambassador-At-Large for Senegal and former President of the African Development Bank, has been a strong advocate for peace and democracy in Africa. Dr. Babacar is currently an ACA Board Member.

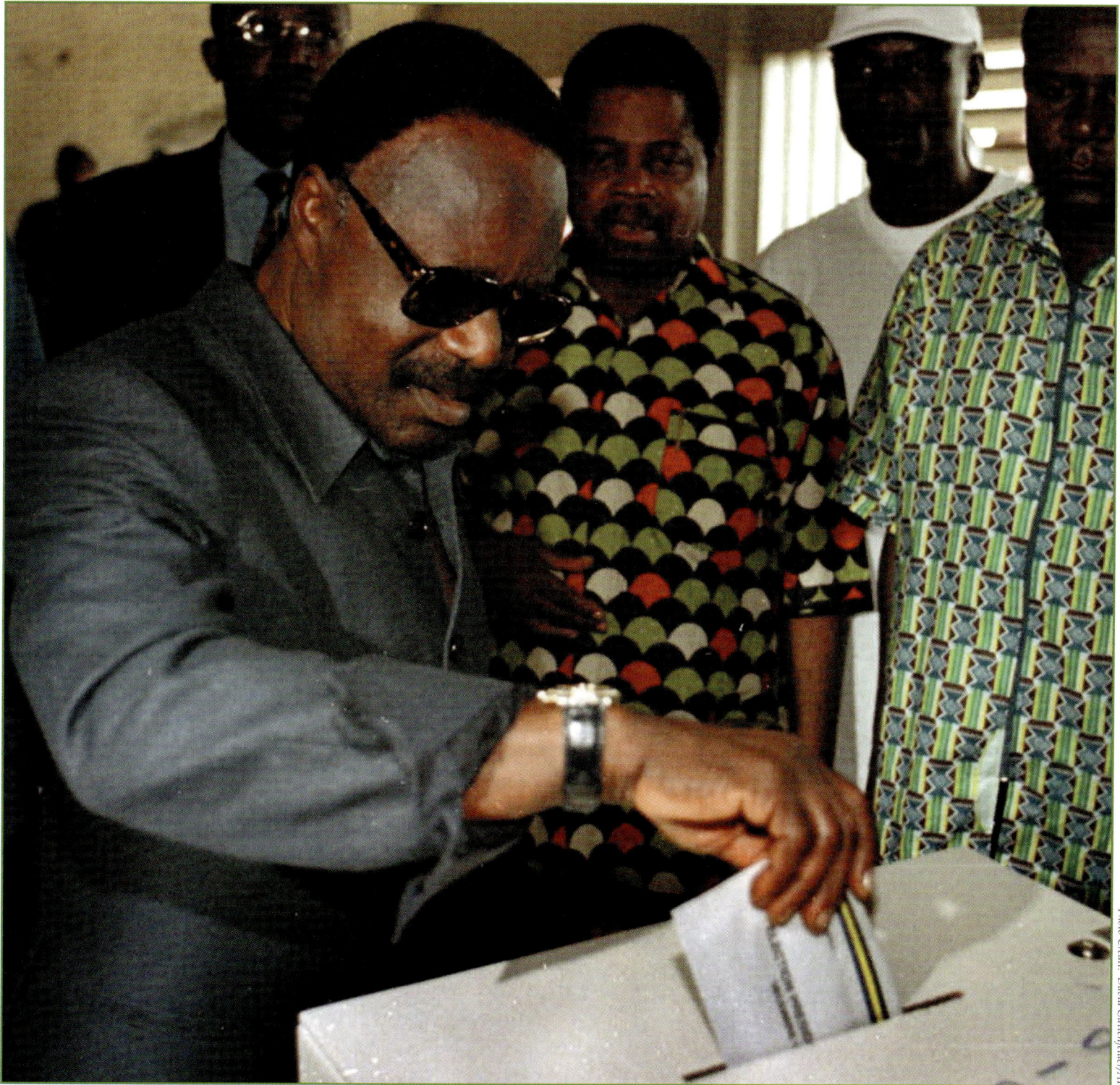

Gabonese President Omar Bongo casts his ballot during the country's presidential elections in Libreville, Gabon. He won overwhelmingly. President Bongo has embraced democracy and encouraged the inclusion of all parties. He has also been the mediator of several conflicts on the continent.

Nigeria

Once marred by a reputation of corruption and political backwardness, Nigeria's democratic elections marked a crucial step toward establishing an accountable and transparent government in a country that has seen eight coups in the 40 years since its independence. A series of local, state, national assembly, and presidential elections were held between December 1998 and February 1999. Retired General Olusegun Obasanjo won the presidential election with nearly 63 percent of the vote and was sworn in on May 29, 1999.

As directed by President Clinton, an Inter-Agency Assessment Team, composed of eight U.S. government agencies visited Nigeria after the elections. Over a two-week period, the team met with President Obasanjo and other Nigerian government officials, civil society leaders, and the American and Nigerian business communities to discuss how the United States could best assist Nigeria with its political, economic and social transformation. Prior to President Clinton's visit, the team reported its findings and recommendations to the President and Congress.

During President Clinton's historic visit to Nigeria, he and President Obasanjo affirmed U.S.-Nigeria

President Clinton greets President Obasanjo during his visit to Washington, D.C.

President Clinton talks with Nigerian President Obasanjo upon arrival in Abuja.

14

relations by signing a Joint Declaration that list human rights and democracy as the first principle in a document containing 17 principles. "Both Presidents agree that their countries share the common goals of promoting human rights and democracy, throughout Africa and the world," the Joint Declaration states. Other Declaration principles address international debt, regional security issues, poverty alleviation, health issues, education, transportation, telecommunications and infrastructure, and private investment and trade.

With a population of more than 100 million people, diverse natural and human resources, enormous economic potential, an active and free press, and a growing and vibrant society, Nigeria has the potential to be the economic engine and

President Clinton signs a Joint Declaration with Nigerian President Obasanjo.

stabilizing influence in West Africa and for much of the rest of Africa. In fact, Nigeria is already a force in the region having taken the lead in creating the Economic Community of West African States (ECOWAS) and later the formation of the Economic Community of West African States Monitoring Group (ECOMOG).

Nigeria is extremely important to the United States. It is the source of 8 percent of America's crude oil imports, more than what is imported from Kuwait, according to the U.S. State Department.

President Clinton greets the children of Ushafa Village in Nigeria.

President Clinton greets Nigeria's First Lady Chief Stella Obasanjo.

President Clinton and Chelsea walking through the village with Nigerian children.

The key reason President Clinton wanted to visit Nigeria was because of Nigeria's importance to the region. We believe the United States can and must continue to build a strong partnership with a democratic Nigeria. A partnership based on shared values, on shared development and economic interest. A commitment to work together on issues of regional and international security. And this is about conveying to the people of Nigeria that the U.S. wants to stand four square beside them as they make this very difficult but vital transition from a dictatorial government to democratic government.

Susan Rice
Assistant Secretary of State
Bureau of African Affairs
U.S. Department of State
Remarks from the OSTR
African Growth and
Opportunity Act Video

President Clinton addresses a Joint Session of the Nigerian National Assembly.

President Clinton and his daughter, Chelsea, accept gifts during a Ceremony in Abuja, Nigeria.

President Clinton and President Obasanjo at the State Dinner at the International Conference Center in Abuja, Nigeria.

"

You were not born with a silver spoon in your mouth, but in these eight years you worked hard to put a silver spoon in the hands and mouths of most Americans. These are reasons why the American people love you, especially combined with your personal charm and grace, generously given with so much bonhomie.

But we have many more reasons to salute you, President Clinton. Your trip here today represents the care and concern you have for the whole of Africa and for all peoples of African descent at home in the U.S. and elsewhere.

The claim of being the first black President of the United States is most endearing, and I dare say, quite befitting. For us, on this visit you have come home. We welcome you, and tonight we confer upon you three Nigerian names in one, to reflect your love for the people, your indomitable courage, and your glorious homecoming. Mr. President, we name you Sodangi, Okoro, Omowale.

President Obasanjo
State Dinner
International
Conference Center
Abuja, Nigeria
August 26, 2000

"

South Africa

The election of President Nelson Mandela following South Africa's peaceful transition from apartheid to multiparty democracy was one of the most important events of the 20th century. A political activist whose opposition to apartheid in South Africa led to his imprisonment for 27 years, President Mandela stands as an example to all who struggle against tyranny in support of freedom. He worked tirelessly to support racial reconciliation among his people and, only four years after his liberation, became the first democratically elected President of South Africa on May 9, 1994.

On September 23, 1998, President Clinton presented President Mandela with one of America's highest honors, the Congressional Gold Medal.

Photo Credit: Ruth Fremson/AP

South African President Nelson Mandela receives applause after he was presented the Congressional Gold Medal. From left are House Minority Leader Richard Gephardt, then House Speaker Newt Gingrich, Mandela and President Clinton.

"President Clinton is a friend of South Africa and Africa," said President Mandela at a White House reception in his honor. "You helped us long before you became president and you have continued with that help now as the president of the greatest country in the world."

The people of South Africa held their second democratic election on June 2, 1999, marking a smooth transfer of power. Under the leadership of President Mandela and, now, President Thabo Mbeki, the government of South Africa has fostered the difficult and lengthy process of national reconciliation and laid the groundwork for long-term political, economic and social reformations.

In the first three years of the Clinton-Gore administration, the United States provided more than $600 million to the newly elected democratic government of South Africa to support democracy and development.

During the President's visit, a Memorandum of Understanding was signed between the Regional Center for Southern Africa and the South African Development Community Parliamentary Forum. The document expresses mutual intent to establish a long-term relationship, one that provides support to the SADC Parliamentary Forum for its programs to strengthen democratic values and processes in Southern Africa. Program areas include developing model legislation to improve the free and fair elections in the region; establishing an electoral monitoring capability on the part of the Parliamentary Forum; and conducting hearings on issues of regional significance or interest.

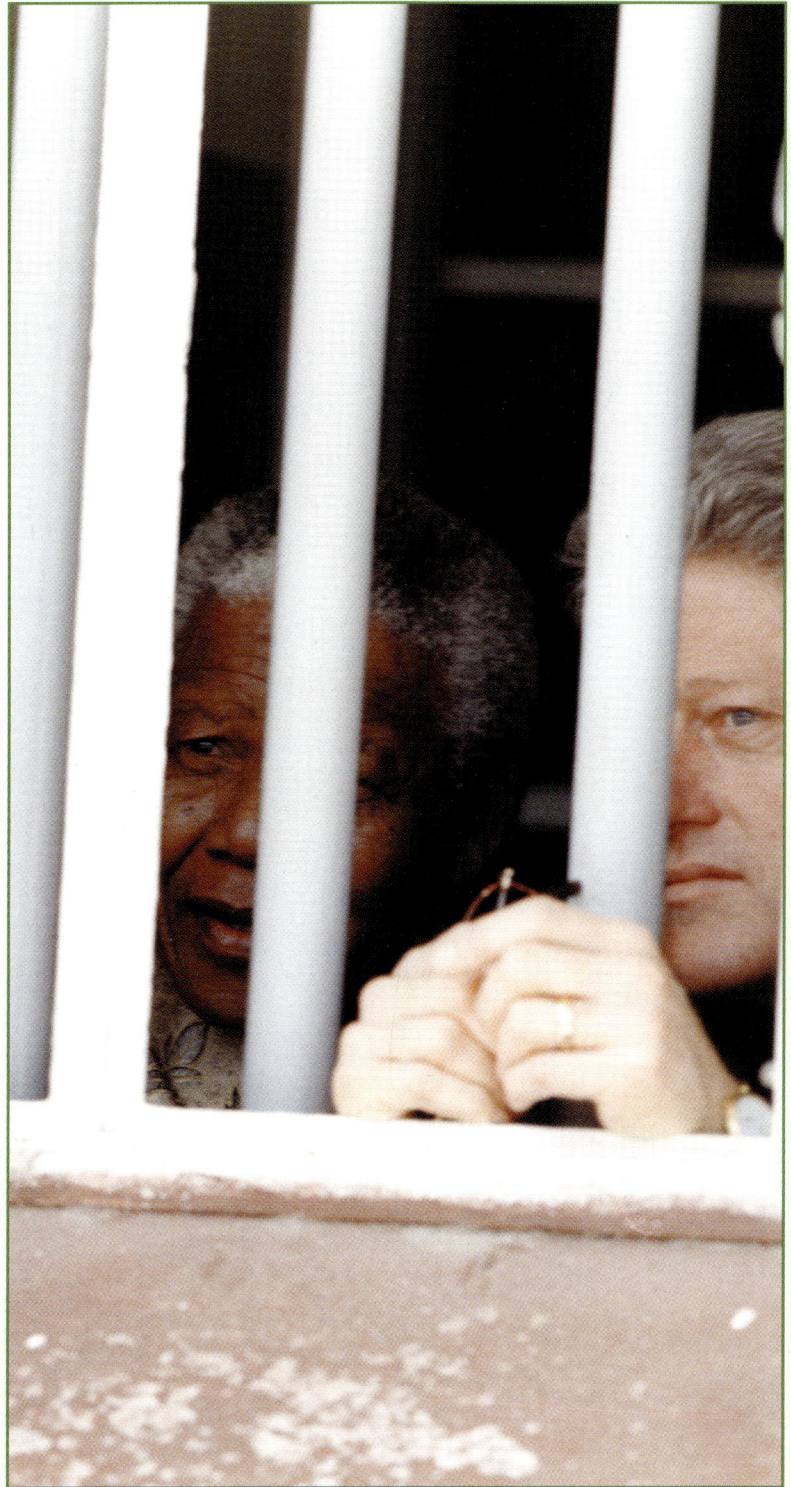

Photo Credit: Sharon Farmer/The White House

President Clinton visits Robben Island, the prison where former South African President Nelson Mandela was held for 27 years.

President Clinton and First Lady Hillary Rodham Clinton host a State Dinner for President Mbeki and First Lady Zanele Mbeki of South Africa on May 22, 2000.

President Clinton and First Lady Hillary Rodham Clinton host a White House State Dinner in honor of South African President Thabo Mbeki and First Lady Zanele Mbeki on May 22, 2000.

President Clinton gives a press conference with South African President Nelson Mandela in Johannesburg.

President Clinton addresses the South African Parliament.

President Clinton and First Lady Hillary Rodham Clinton join a woman laying bricks during a visit to the Victoria Mxenge housing project in Guguletu, South Africa, a USAID funded program where women build their homes.

I don't remember any experience in my life more exciting than going to Accra in Ghana (with the President in 1998). I had been there. I knew that city. To suddenly see 700,000 people coming out to see the President of the United States. You realize how much good feeling there was there — the good feeling and the opportunity, the desire to be involved with us and the respect they have for the President. There were many impressions.

Over and over again you were impressed by the fact that President Clinton was known about and was liked and they were eager to get involved with us. If nothing else came out of that trip, it was important for people to see on television this picture because so much of what Americans know about Africa is related to disasters or wars or very upsetting scenes. This was a positive kind of scene of what is really possible in those countries. For that reason, the President put Africa in a good light. That was another real positive thing that came out of it. That's something that only he could do.

Congressman
James McDermott
(R-WA)
ACA Interview

Photo Credit: Sharon Farmer/The White House

President Clinton addresses the people of Ghana with First Lady Hillary Rodham Clinton and President Jerry John Rawlings of Ghana and First Lady Nana Konadu Agyeman-Rawlings.

Ghana

Ghana is a key ally of the United States. With successful multiparty elections completed in December 1996, Ghana is now in the forefront of African countries that have made positive steps toward consolidating democracy. The historic elections — the first held under a democratically elected government — were recognized by the international community as being free, fair and transparent and expressing the will of Ghana's 18 million citizens.

During his 1998 visit to Ghana, President Clinton announced the United States would donate $500,000 under the International Criminal Investigative and Training Assistance Program

(ICITAP) of the U.S. Department of Justice to assist the Ghanaian police force in improving and strengthening its non-lethal crowd control capabilities; increasing professional officer training; and enhancing organizational, structural, and managerial resources. ICITAP helps countries train and educate police forces through educational programs that address the role of police in a democracy, community policing, and human dignity.

In support of Ghana's role in peacekeeping, the United States also finalized an agreement with the Ghanaian government to receive six modern military helicopters in 2000 for the Ghanaian armed forces under the excess defense articles program. As part of this program, President Clinton is authorized to transfer excess defense equipment to countries that exhibit peacekeeping efforts.

Photo Credit: Ralph Alswang/The White House

President Clinton and First Lady Hillary Rodham Clinton arrive at Kotoka International Airport in Accra, Ghana.

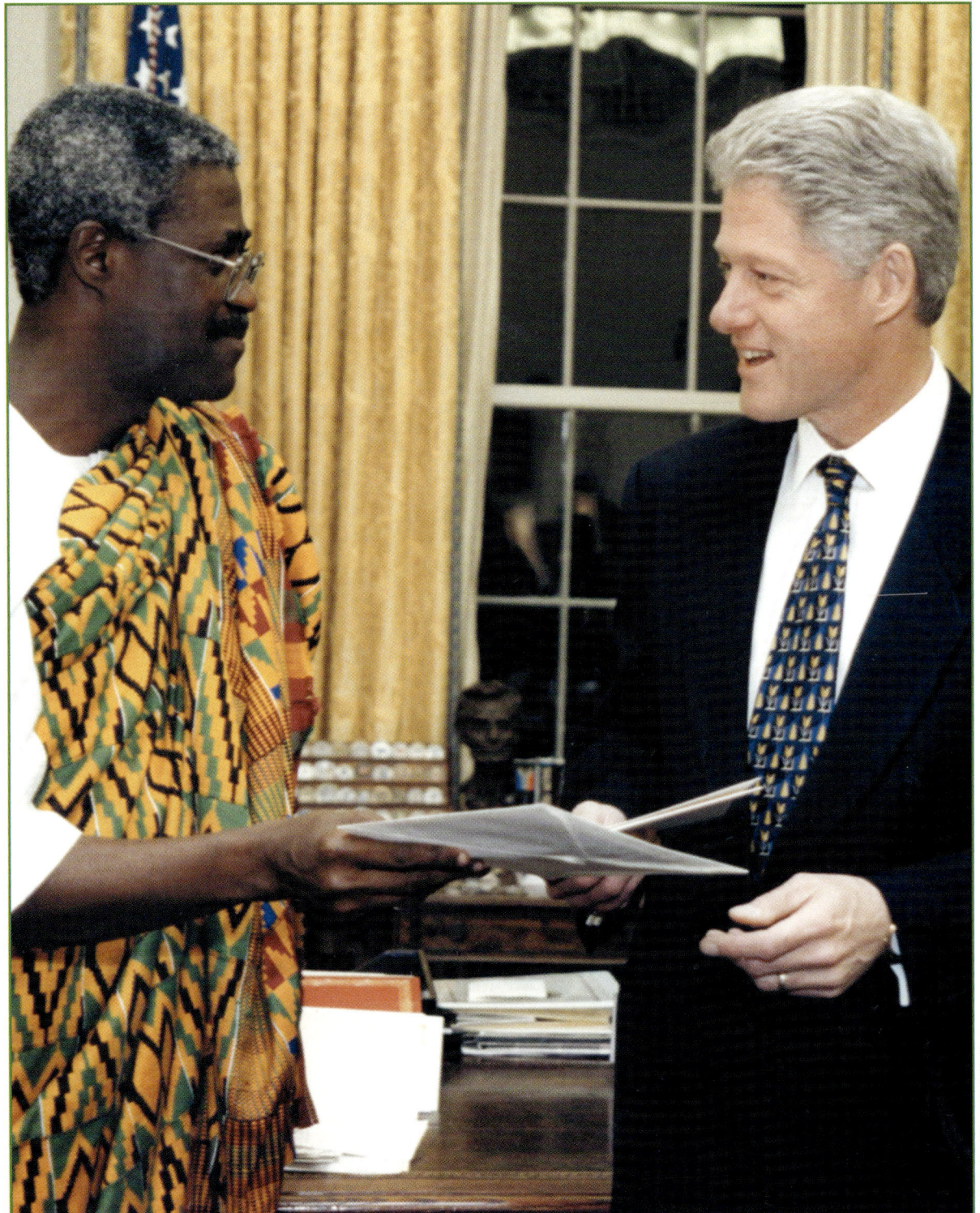

President Clinton in the Oval Office with Ambassador Koby Arthur Koomson of Ghana.

Photo Credit: The White House

28

President Clinton and President Rawlings at the White House State Dinner on February 24, 1999.

President Rawlings of Ghana delivers his remarks at the White House State Dinner in his honor on February 24, 1999.

Let me say that as short as this visit is, I think what's most important is the content. And there's no doubt that the agenda that's been drawn out would be an issue that takes on the serious subjects that concern Africa, an issue that's been initiated by the President and members of his Cabinet. That's most welcome to this continent.

Let me remind you, ladies and gentlemen, 27 years from now, as I said to some of our colleagues in the CNN yesterday, that the population of this continent or sub-Saharan Africa will be doubling to about 1.5 billion. And if we don't take the appropriate measures both from the economic standpoint and the political standpoint, to lay the foundation towards development and peace, I'm afraid we'll be running down the hill.

However, I feel very hopeful and very confident that the measures we've taken and a good numbers of African countries, we're beginning to register a healthy economic upturn. The political stability that's returning to this continent, no doubt, I believe is what must have encouraged the President and his colleagues to take on this issue and to do what they can to assist the efforts that we're putting in Africa.

President Jerry Rawlings Remarks During Photo Opportunity with President Clinton Osu Castle Garden Accra, Ghana March 23, 1998

Photo Credit: Bob McNeely/The White House

President Clinton tours Osu Castle with President Rawlings of Ghana.

Photo Credit: Chris Pizzello/AP

Singer Michael Jackson hugs President Jerry Rawlings of Ghana at a welcoming banquet for Rawlings at the Beverly Hilton Hotel in Beverly Hills, California. Jackson presented Rawlings with two gold swords on behalf of Saudi Arabian Prince Alwaleed Bin Talal Al-Saudi. At left in the photo is Dr. Khalid Abdullah Tariq Al-Mansour, ACA Board Member. A number of celebrities from the United States have visited Ghana.

Rwanda

We should not have allowed the refugee camps to become safe havens for killers. We did not immediately call these crimes by their rightful name: genocide. We cannot change the past. But we can and must do everything in our power to help you build a future without fear, and full of hope. We owe to those who died and to those who survived who loved them, our every effort to increase our vigilance and strengthen our stand against those who could commit such atrocities in the future - - here or elsewhere.

President William Jefferson Clinton
Address to Genocide Survivors
Kigali, Rwanda
March 25, 1998

In Rwanda, up to one million people were massacred in less than four months as a result of genocide that swept through the country in 1994. Families were murdered in their homes, and people hunted down as they fled soldiers and militia through farmland and woods. People often sought refuge in schools, hospitals, and churches. However, if they were found, they were killed simply because their identity card said they were Tutsi or because they had a Tutsi parent. Some were even killed because they were Hutus who looked like Tutsis or because they protected Tutsis.

During President Clinton's 1998 visit to Rwanda, he acknowledged that "the international community, together with nations in Africa, must bear its share of responsibility for this tragedy." To begin the process of healing and restoring peace, the President announced an initial $2 million contribution to the Genocide Survivor's Fund. The United States was the first country to contribute to the Genocide Survivor's Fund and is one of the largest contributors to the International Criminal Tribunal for Rwanda. The U.S. Agency for International Development paid school fees for three years for 2,500 students as part of the Genocide Survivor's Fund.

The Joint Declaration of Principles signed during the Entebbe Summit for Peace and Prosperity also "condemns all acts of genocide and pledges to undertake a concerted effort to prevent its resurgence." The Declaration further states that "the United States commits itself through the Great Lakes Justice Initiative to an expanded effort to help the public and private sectors in Rwanda, Burundi and the Democratic Republic of Congo develop justice systems that are impartial, credible, and effective, and to support efforts to promote inclusion, coexistence, cooperation and security."

Photo Credit: Greg Gibson/AP

President Clinton and Rwandan President Pasteur Bizimungu and Rwandan First Lady Serafin Bizimungu and U.S. First Lady Hillary Rodham Clinton walk together at the Kigali, Rwanda airport.

President Clinton looks at a sculpture presented to him representing the 1994 genocide in Kigali, Rwanda.

Liberia

Liberia's seven-year civil war ended with the free and transparent election of President Charles Taylor on July 19, 1997. Many Liberians had been forced to flee their country due to civil war and widespread violence. While the civil war is over, the United States is concerned about Liberia's role in the war in Sierra Leone.

On October 11, 2000, President Clinton signed a proclamation calling on the "Liberian government to end immediately Liberia's trafficking in weapons and illicit diamonds, which fuels the war in Sierra Leone, and instead to use its influence with the Revolutionary United Front (RUF) to restore peace and stability to Sierra Leone. Members of my Administration have repeatedly made this request of President Taylor. The absence of any positive response from his government leaves us little choice but to impose these restrictions. Only when the Government of Liberia ends its participation in activities that support the RUF will the United States review this policy."

The proclamation suspends the entry into the United States, as immigrants and non-immigrants, of all persons — and their spouses, children, and parents - who plan, engage in, or benefit from activities that support the RUF, or that otherwise impede the peace process in Sierra Leone.

On September 28, 2000, President Clinton also directed the U.S. Attorney General and the Immigration and Naturalization Service to defer for one year the deportation of certain Liberians living in the United States.

"I am concerned that a decision by our government to deport Liberians who have enjoyed protection of our country for so many years could cause the involuntary repatriation of many thousands of Liberian refugees from other nations in West Africa," said President Clinton. "This would severely burden Liberia and cause instability in Liberia and in the region."

During the Clinton Administration, spending on U.S. efforts in conflict resolution also increased. The United States spent nearly $100 million to support regional peacekeeping efforts by the Economic Community of West African States' peacekeeping operation and humanitarian relief efforts in Sierra Leone and Liberia. The U.S. government has given almost $8 million to the Organization of African Unity (OAU) to build and equip a Crisis Management Center at its headquarters in Addis Ababa, Ethiopia.

Her Excellency Ruth Perry, former interim President of Liberia.

White House Conference on Africa

President Clinton's efforts to improve U.S.-Africa relations were not conceived haphazardly or in a vacuum. In June 1994, he convened the first ever White House Conference on Africa. This conference brought members of the Administration together with 150 of America's leaders on African affairs, including experts from Congress, business, labor, religious groups, human rights groups, academia, environmental groups and others to discuss critical African issues and the U.S. response to them.

In announcing the conference, the President said, "The challenges facing Africa and American policy towards the continent will draw on the participation and combined efforts of all Americans. This meeting is an important opportunity for leaders who care deeply about Africa to share ideas and experiences." Among the issues discussed were the promotion of sustainable development, responses to internal conflicts, support for democracy and human rights, and enhancing bilateral trade and investment ties.

Photo Courtesy of ACA

Archbishop and Mrs. Desmond Tutu with ACA producer Tony Regusters at Nelson Mandela's 80th birthday celebration in Johannesburg.

Photo Credit: George Bridges/AP

President Clinton greets Organization of Africa Unity Secretary General Salim Salim during the opening session of the on U.S.-Africa Ministerial Conference, as U.S. Secretary of State Madeleine Albright and Assistant Secretary of State Susan Rice look on.

President Clinton addresses the U.S.-Africa Ministerial Conference on March 16, 1999.

The U.S.-Africa Ministerial Conference

In 1999, the United States hosted the first meeting of African and American officials to enhance the U.S.-Africa partnership by addressing greater political reform, economic development, trade, investment, and mutual economic growth in the 21st century. President Clinton, eight members of his Cabinet, and four agency heads met for the first time with African delegations from across the continent. Eighty-three ministers from 46 sub-Saharan African nations, representatives from four North African nations, and the heads of eight African regional organizations participated in this historic meeting.

In an effort to consolidate and build on the significant progress achieved in Africa in recent years, ministers and senior U.S. officials discussed concrete ways to accelerate Africa's integration into the global economy. The African Ministers expressed strong support for the African Growth and Opportunity Act and for continued implementation of the President's Partnership for Economic Growth and Opportunity. U.S. and African officials engaged in an active exchange on a broad range of economic, political, and social issues.

The Ministerial adopted "The Blueprint for Partnership," which detailed the way forward for future U.S.-Africa cooperation. The Blueprint summarizes the frank and open dialogue on a range of economic, political, and social issues.

President Clinton and Ambassador Joseph Diatta, from the Republic of Niger.

During the Ministerial, U.S. Trade Representative Ambassador Charlene Barshefsky also chaired the first comprehensive roundtable with African trade ministers on the World Trade Organization (WTO). The roundtable was co-chaired by the Organization of African Unity/African Economic Committee.

Ugandan President Yoweri Museveni, standing, who was one of the facilitators of the Burundi Peace Talks, addresses delegates in Arusha, Tanzania.

Photo Credit: Sayyid Azim/AP

Burundi Peace Talks

Peace and democracy are the cornerstone of President Clinton's partnership initiative. Therefore, President Clinton and several administration officials personally participated in the Burundi Peace Talks. The peace process began with the Arusha peace negotiations, initiated under the leadership of late Tanzanian President Julius Nyerere in 1996. Dr. Nyerere and the parties made considerable progress, and talks were given new impetus in December, when former South African President Nelson Mandela was appointed as facilitator to replace Nyerere, who died in October 1999. President Mandela also organized a February 2000 plenary session in Arusha that was attended by all 18 parties. Several regional leaders joined him at the February 21 opening

President Clinton addresses the Burundi Peace Talks in Arusha. He also addressed the February plenary session via satellite.

Photo Credit: William Vasta/The White House

session, and at the request of President Mandela, President Clinton addressed the closing session via satellite.

Burundi's recent history has been marked by a destructive struggle between the Tutsi minority and the Hutu majority that has been excluded from political and economic opportunities. Burundi's first democratically elected president, Melchior Ndadye, a Hutu, was assassinated in 1993. Since then, more than 200,000 Burundians have been killed in clashes between Tutsi-dominated governments and Hutu rebels. Hundreds of thousands have been internally displaced or become refugees in neighboring countries, and the Burundi economy has continued to crumble. President Pierre Buyoya, a Tutsi who was the head of state from 1987 to 1993, and returned to power in a bloodless coup d'état in July 1996.

In August 2000, former South African President Nelson Mandela invited President Clinton to participate in the Burundi Peace Talks in Arusha, Tanzania. Addressing the group on the 37th anniversary of the March on Washington, President Clinton invoked the lives of Dr. Martin L. King Jr. and President Mandela as examples of how rising above hatred, greed, and power always prevails. He aptly stated, "...everybody needs a dream, and I think whether you all decide to sign this or not depends in part on what your dream is. Sooner or later hatred, vengeance, the illusion that power over another group of people will bring security in life, these feelings can be just as iron, just as confining as the doors of a prison cell."

Following the meetings and peace talks, the parties signed an agreement that enabled them to resolve outstanding issues, including cease-fire and transitional leadership.

Photo Credit: J. Scott Applewhite/AP

Surrounded by African leaders and Burundi peace negotiators, President Clinton and former South African President Nelson Mandela shake hands following the Burundi Peace Talks in Arusha, Tanzania.

President Clinton jokes with Uganda's President Yoweri Museveni at a press conference following the Entebbe Summit for Peace and Prosperity in Entebbe, Uganda.

Photo Credit: Greg Gibson/AP

Entebbe Summit for Peace and Prosperity

On March 25, 1998, President Clinton played a vital role in the Entebbe Summit for Peace and Prosperity. At the joint invitation of President Clinton and President Yoweri Kaguta Museveni of the Republic of Uganda, five African heads of state and Salim Ahmed Salim, Secretary General of the Organization of African Unity, met and signed a Joint Declaration of Principles on issues ranging from conflict resolution and democracy to economic reform.

The participating heads of state included: their excellencies Daniel T. Arap Moi, President of the Republic of Kenya; Pasteur Bizimungu, President of the Republic of Rwanda; Benjamin William Mkapa, President of the United Republic of Tanzania; Laurent Desire Kabila, President of the Democratic Republic of Congo; and Meles Zenawi, Prime Minister of the Federal Democratic Republic of Ethiopia. The exchange of views between President Clinton and the African leaders marked a new beginning, launching a process of defining and building the U.S.-Africa Partnership for the 21st Century.

The presidents signed a Joint Declaration of Principles affirming that "Africa and the United States hold a mutual interest in fostering Africa's economic and political transformation and full integration into the global economy, and in promoting democratic participation and respect for human rights." And, moreover, that "social, economic and political inclusion is the foundation for lasting peace and stability."

The Declaration further states that "African and American security interests alike will be advanced by a joint attack on the transnational problems of terrorism, disease, proliferation of weapons, drug trafficking and environmental degradation."

Clinton watches African leaders sign an agreement on the prevention of genocide, at the Entebbe Summit for Peace and Prosperity.

African Crisis Response Initiative

The African Crisis Response Initiative (ACRI) was launched in 1996 to enhance the capacity of African countries to respond quickly and effectively to peacekeeping and humanitarian relief contingencies on the continent. The objectives of ACRI are to train approximately 12,000 peacekeepers; build effective command and control; provide commonality and interoperability; and enhance international, regional and sub-regional peacekeeping capacity in Africa.

ACRI has conducted battalion initial training in Senegal, Uganda, Malawi, Mali, Ghana, Kenya, Benin and Côte d'Ivoire.

During battalion initial training, U.S. Army instructors train African soldiers in a highly professional program of instruction in peacekeeping and humanitarian relief operations. Six months after initial training, follow-on training begins and continues every six months for two and a half

President Clinton is saluted by American troops during a visit to Thies Military Base, Senegal. The American soldiers are training with the Senegalese forces in preparation for joint peacekeeping and other operations.

Photo Credit: J. Scott Applewhite/AP

years. Observance of human rights is reinforced throughout the training program.

ACRI has provided training and non-lethal equipment (including uniforms, boots, generators, mine detectors, night vision devices, and water purification units) to almost 6,000 peacekeepers. Training is based on the "train-the-trainer" concept. ACRI also incorporates a briefing on HIV/AIDS in the military in all training events.

ACRI has contributed to conflict resolution in Africa, where several partner countries have made sovereign decisions to deploy peacekeepers in international operations. Mali and Ghana sent forces to Sierra Leone as part of the Economic Community of West African States (ECOWAS) peacekeeping force. Benin sent a contingent to Guinea-Bissau, and Senegalese peacekeepers were engaged under the UN mission in the Central African Republic. Malawi and Senegal also prepared ACRI-trained contingents for duty in the Democratic Republic of the Congo.

In March 1999, the U.S. Department of Defense also launched the African Center for Strategic Studies, a two-week Senior Leader Seminar that provides a rigorous academic and practical program in civil-military relations, national security strategy and defense economics. President Clinton announced his intention to establish the Center during his March 1998 Africa trip.

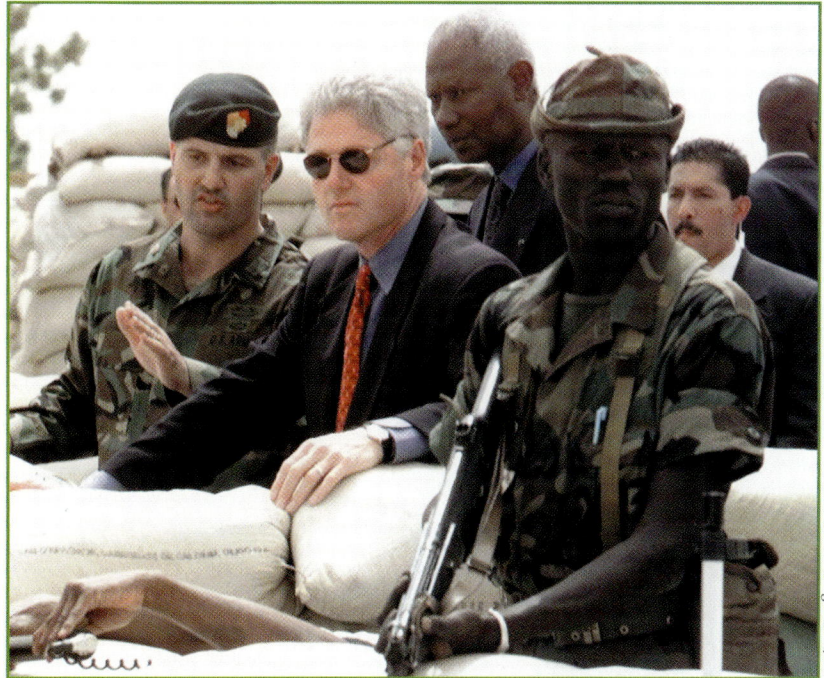

Photo Credit: Greg Gibson/AP

U.S. President Clinton, and former Senegal's President Abdou Diouf, third left, listen to an explanation by Major Adrian Erckenbrack, with U.S. Special Forces out of Fort Bragg while watching Senegalese troops during peacekeeping training at Thies Military Base.

Photo Credit: J. Scott Applewhite/AP

President Bill Clinton talks to Major Erckenbrack with U.S. Special Forces behind a sandbag parapet during peacekeeping training for Senegalese forces at Thies Military Base, Senegal. Congressman Charles Rangel (D-NY) looks on.

> The legacy of President Clinton is a legacy of friendship first. We see him like a great President and colorblind. You see that in his Cabinet. We see that in his visits. He could visit any country in Africa and we see him as the President.
>
> The Senegalese government decided not to let him speak at the capital in Dakar but symbolically on the Goree Island side. Something that struck us all was when he said this was the place where slaves left involuntarily to go to the United States. And he went on to say today, there is the return of many leaders like Secretary Slater, Jesse Jackson, and Congressman Rangel. I was very proud of him to say that.
>
> *Ambassador Seck*
> *Ambassador of Senegal*
> *ACA Interview*

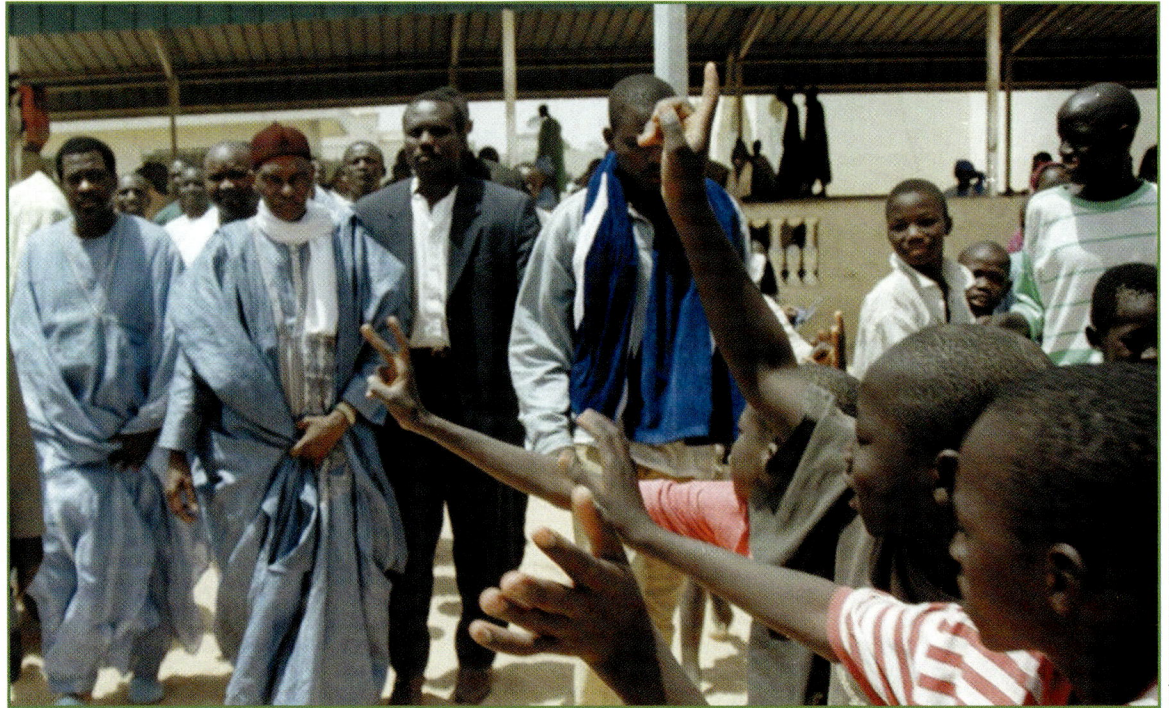

President-elect Abodoulae Wade, second left, leaves the palace of the leader of Senegal's 2-million strong Mouride brotherhood in Touba, more than 120 miles east of the capital, during a pilgrimage to thank Islamic leaders following his win in Senegal's election.

Photo Credit: Moustahia Ba/AP

President Clinton greets Ambassador Mamadou Seck of Senegal to the United States.

Photo Credit: White House Photo/Courtesy of the Embassy of Senegal

The Great Lakes Justice Initiative

In Rwanda, President Clinton announced the United States would invest $30 million in the Great Lakes Justice Initiative (GLJI) to help develop justice systems that are impartial, credible and effective. The United States will work as a partner with the people and the governments of the region to support judicial systems. The region includes Rwanda, Burundi, and the Democratic Republic of the Congo.

For too long, the region of the Great Lakes had been caught in a deepening cycle of violence and anarchy that often spilled over national and ethnic boundaries. Ethnic tensions and political and economic failures have resulted in bloodshed, instability, and economic ruin. For the people of the Great Lakes region to escape this vicious cycle, there must be a concerted effort to construct effective systems of justice and a move toward reconciliation.

Following a process of consultations with interested African governments and civil society organizations, this initiative targets: judicial planning bodies such as the Ministries of Justice and Interior; the functions of court systems, prosecu-

Photo Courtesy of ACA

Attorney General and Minister of Justice, Chief Bola Ige, S.A.N. of the Federal Republic of Nigeria attends a ministerial conference in Arizona. Chief Ige is working very hard to ensure that his ministry supports these types of initiatives.

tors, police and prison systems; national officials; support for police and judiciary; court administration systems through pilot projects; and viable plans for their system-wide replication; bar associations, universities and commercial and professional organizations; military personnel; and demobilization of irregular elements of standing armies and their reintegration into society and programs to demobilize child soldiers.

Greater Horn of Africa Initiative

In 1994, President Clinton launched the Greater Horn of Africa Initiative (GHAI) to address the recurring cycle of crisis, instability and famine in the Greater Horn of Africa region by improving food security and establishing a system of conflict early warning, prevention and response. As a presidential initiative, GHAI operates under the direct authority and policy guidance of the president and the secretary of state. The USAID Administrator is the designated head of the Initiative.

The Greater Horn of Africa region comprises Eritrea, Ethiopia, Sudan, Somalia, Djibouti, Kenya, Uganda, Tanzania, Rwanda and Burundi. Conflict in this region is usually, directly or indirectly, related to access to land and water — the primary productive resources of the region.

Perhaps the Initiative's most effective tools are that the principles are guided by African ownership and participation, strategic coordination, linking relief to development, analyzing and responding to events within the context of a regional perspective, and planning in advance preparedness.

Photo Credit: Courtesy of the Embassy of Uganda

President Clinton greets Felicia Ssempala, as her mother Ambassador Edith Ssempala of Uganda looks on. Uganda participates in the Greater Horn of Africa Initiative.

President Clinton addresses the Congressional Black Caucus Foundation Dinner in front of a backdrop showing slain civil rights leader Martin Luther King, Jr., who was a drum major for peace and justice in the United States and around the world.

President Clinton is extremely popular in Africa. I think he started becoming popular very shortly after his Inauguration. When Africans took a look at his Cabinet, they liked what they saw. I remember him promising that he would have a Cabinet that would look like America. He did. The presentation of blacks, in particular, was very impressive to Africans.

As you know, Africa is not a place that U.S. Presidents go to. The rhetoric from Washington under the Clinton Administration has been popular. President Clinton is perceived by Africans to have worked hard for debt relief, for the emancipation of South Africa, and for trying as much as possible to bring investments into Africa.

African journalists also have a favorable response about the President. Even though he is likable, he has great communication skills. Clinton is very understandable. As a journalist and an African, I think Clinton is great!

Somebody once joked that Clinton is actually black. He may have white skin but his heart is definitely black. Clinton is one American politician who has succeeded in establishing a rapport with the diverse groups of the United States, particularly with blacks. And I think he has popularized the Democratic Party within the black community by the way he interacts with black people not only in the United States but worldwide.

At Voice of America, we deal with issues that are important and of interest to them – politics, agriculture, education, sports, everything. And we tell them the truth. It may be good, it may be bad but, we tell them the truth. We don't advertise or sell anything. We only inform. So people have gotten used to waking up to Voice of America in all parts of the world. The idea of Voice of America not being there is not even imaginable. It doesn't even come into their minds. It's part of a lifestyle for a lot of people around the world.

The radio is still the major form of communication throughout Africa because television isn't as widely available as it is in the west. You go into the bush, you see people walking around with radio transistors. At 9 or 9:30 a.m., you hear sounds coming in from Washington, D.C. They are so well informed. Not only are they well informed, they are also very attentive to what's going on around the world. Our job is to tell them what's happening. Their job is to make up their minds on what to do with the information they receive from us.

Aliyu Mustapha
International Broadcaster
Voice of America
ACA Interview

Radio Democracy for Africa

In 1998, President Clinton announced the establishment of Radio Democracy for Africa. Through this initiative, the people of Africa receive an additional 22.5 hours per week of programs focused primarily on democracy and human rights throughout the continent. Radio Democracy reporters report on statements by politicians and political leaders of various orientations.

Due to the repressive media climate in some countries, foreign reporters are now able to cover such stories without fear of reprisal. Radio Democracy also focuses on promoting conflict resolution by covering reconciliation efforts.

Photo Credit: Clint Karlsen/AP

Federal Communications Commission Chairman Bill Kennard addresses the National Association of Broadcasters convention.

Vusi Sixhaso, a founding member of Radio Zibonele, conducts a program in his studio in September of 1995 in Cape Town, South Africa.

President Clinton and Nigerian President Obasanjo at a press conference following the signing of the Joint Declaration in Abuja, Nigeria.

Fostering
Trade *and*
Economic
Development

Last year, our growing relationship with this enormous market helped to protect the United States from the global financial crisis raging elsewhere. While exports were down in other parts of the world, exports from the United States to Africa actually went up by eight percent, topping $6 billion. As wise investors have discovered, investments in Africa pay. In 1997, the rate of return of American investments in Africa was 36 percent — compared with 16 percent in Asia, 14 percent worldwide, 11 percent in Europe.

President William Jefferson Clinton
U.S.-Africa Ministerial Conference
U.S. Department of State
March 16, 1999

As the world increasingly embraced global trade in the 1990's, an important part of the puzzle was missing – Africa. President Clinton told Congress, leaders of industrialized nations, the United Nations, and the World Trade Organization that trade is not global if Africa, which accounts for one-fifth of the world's population, is ignored. And, with seeds securely planted by the late Secretary of Commerce Ronald Brown encouraging him to visit Africa and explore its enormous opportunities, President Clinton began a historic new chapter in U.S.-Africa trade relations.

With vision and tenacity, President Clinton sought to create an "equal partnership," where African heads of state can discuss business and economic development opportunities that benefit Africa and the United States -- a symbiotic relationship that had once been only a pipe dream to observers of and participants in U.S.-Africa policy. A relationship where African countries can depend on America to help them build stable, economically dynamic democratic nations, and where quality of life is more important than the continent's natural resources.

President Clinton's trade and economic development initiatives in Africa shed light on America's historically "do nothing" strategy. Acknowledging America's lack of or failed Africa policies, President Clinton launched the historic Partnership for Economic Growth and Opportunity in Africa Initiative. The success of the Partnership in fostering trade and economic development in Africa is unparalleled -- the first Africa trade bill passed by the U.S. Congress, the first trade agreements with South Africa and Ghana, the first

Photo Credit: Courtesy of Women's Center, Abuja

Exhibition for the visit of President Clinton to the National Centre for Women Development in Abuja, Nigeria.

Assistant U.S. Trade Representative for Africa, and the first Presidential Business Development Mission.

Several U.S. companies are already realizing Africa's potential. U.S. trade with sub-Saharan Africa has grown on average by 16.9 percent annually since 1994, outpacing growth in global trade in 1995 and 1996, according to the Office of the U.S. Trade Representative. U.S. exports to Africa reached $6.2 billion in 1997, while African exports to the United States -- 70 percent of which are crude oil -- totaled $16.4 billion. Africa's $10.2 billion trade surplus with the United States in 1997 accrued almost entirely to oil exporters.

A major part of President Clinton's Partnership is the historic African Growth and Opportunity Act, the first U.S.-Africa trade legislation passed by the United States Congress. The pages that follow will highlight AGOA, the late Secretary of Commerce Ronald H. Brown, debt relief and government agencies participating in the President's Partnership Initiative.

Statistics confirm the massive economic opportunities for businesses on the continent. In 1999, the world's fastest growing economy was Mozambique, and Botswana was second.

Although U.S. exports to the region account for less than 1 percent of total U.S. exports, according to the White House, U.S. exports to Africa now exceed by 20 percent those to all of the former Soviet Union combined.

Partnership for Economic Growth and Opportunity in Africa Initiative

In June 1997, President Clinton launched the Partnership for Economic Growth and Opportunity in Africa Initiative, which serves as the cornerstone of U.S.-Africa policy and offers a comprehensive strategy for promoting trade, investment and development. The goals of the partnership are to support aggressive reform-oriented economic policies that will build strong, capable economic partners in Africa, to expand trade and investment opportunities for America and African companies through greater access to financing, and to ensure passage of the African Growth and Opportunity Act.

As part of the partnership, President Clinton also appointed Rosa Whitaker, the first Assistant U.S. Trade Representative for Africa, with broad responsibilities for coordinating U.S. trade policy. Other achievements include Trade and Investment Framework Agreements with South Africa and Ghana, a Bilateral Investment Treaty with Mozambique, and a new Advisory Committee on Africa at the Export Import Bank.

President Clinton's visits to Africa were more than pomp and circumstance. He was serious about bringing novel ideas and promoting them with agreements, policies and programs that would improve America's new thinking on U.S.-Africa relations. During each country tour, he unveiled initiatives, programs, policies, or agreements that will improve America's partnership with Africa for generations to come.

Photo Credit: Courtesy of ACA

Alhaji Bamanga Tukur, ACA Chairman, is always at work.

"I commend President Clinton for acknowledging the fact that trade and economic development are essential to U.S. policy on Africa. As the vice president of the African Business Roundtable, I have worked over the years to advance this cause. To have President Clinton not only embrace Africa's trade and economic development, but also demonstrate his support on all levels -- in Africa, in Congress, the United Nations, the G-7, the World Trade Organization, the press and general public -- made an enormous difference to the African business community.

While all of his partnership initiatives are important, trade and economic development will pave the way for financial and economic self-sufficiency for Africa and its people in the 21st century and beyond. Some say Africa is the last frontier for trade and investment. As home to the cradle of civilization, we consider it the first frontier. Too often economic opportunities throughout the continent have been exploited for selfish gain, and few if any Africans reaped the benefits. And, all too often our stories of success are never reported in the U.S. media.

We are poised to accept our rightful place in society as innovators, savvy businessmen and women, intellectuals, and wise stewards. We thank President Clinton for his novel approach to U.S.-Africa relations and we look forward to building on his legacy."

Alhaji Bamanga Tukur
Chairman, African
Communications Agency
Vice President
African Business Roundtable

We have dealt with Africa in essentially five stages. The first stage was slavery — 200-plus years in which Africa, through the process, suffered as America's development, where Africa became the creditor and our country the debtor. Two hundred years of work without wages is a subsidy. Two hundred years of raw materials, viable materials, below market rate a subsidy. Many of our earlier Wall Street investment firms were shipping companies importing Africans as slaves and exporting cotton. And so the foundation of our nation's wealth is hugely connected to the first stage of our relationship with Africa.

The second stage was that of neglect, just neglect, the exploited continent — which the President talked about quite a bit today. The third stage was using Africa as a pawn, a manipulative pawn during times of war and times of crisis, with no regard for its being colonized and lack of development — no commitment to bring it in the tent of global policy. The fourth stage was Africa paternalistically, or simply relating to Africa as aid and a kind of gesture toward people who — starvation, whose desperation was embarrassing — we were able to give some aid and did so. The fifth stage, a partnership, is the most mature stage of our development, the most politically sound, the most morally correct. Africa's development and security and our growth is very connected one to the other.

Reverend Jesse Jackson
Press Briefing
Nile Conference Center
Kampala, Uganda
March 24, 1998

For example, during President Clinton's visit to Botswana, three memoranda of understanding (MOU) addressing economic growth were signed between the Southern African Development Community (SADC) and the U.S. government -- the SADC Customs Procedures, the South African Rolling Stock Information System (RSIS), and the Regional Activity to Promote Integration through Dialogue and Policy Implementation (RAPID).

The SADC Customs Procedures will help the 14 SADC countries standardize and improve customs procedures in the region. The $2.2 million agreement will be implemented over a three- to five-year period. At the signing ceremony, it was noted that the agreement "--will make it easier for goods to flow between the countries of Southern Africa. [This is] an important step in the region's continued economic growth and should result in lower prices for a wide range of products."

Former South African President Nelson Mandela, center, talks to the press after meeting with African heads of state in Cape Town.

Vice President Al Gore, left, and his South African counterpart Thabo Mbeki, shake hands as they hand over signed cooperation agreements in Pretoria that will support the Southern African Development Community region.

The RSIS agreement will assist SADC in further implementation of the RSIS, an ongoing $12 million project funded by the U.S. government, enabling the eight SADC railways to operate more efficiently and serve their customers better by allowing them to track their goods across international borders.

RAPID assists governments, regional institutions, and the private sector in Southern Africa to simplify, harmonize, and implement laws, regulations, policies, and procedures that lead to regional economic integration. The MOU added $5.4 million to RAPID.

The African Growth and Opportunity Act

> I think the trade bill signals a new attitude more than anything else. I don't think there is anything in the bill that is overtly dynamic per se, there isn't a heck of a lot of money in the bill but, what it does is signals a different attitude of how America views Africa. From a continent that is dependent on welfare, on aid, food baskets to a continent that has people that have interest that have resources, that we should deal with as partners as we deal with Asia, Latin America, Europe, Russia and other parts of the world. So I see it as a signaling of a different attitude from America to Africa.
>
> Ron Brown really established the economic link. This trade bill grew out of Ron's legacy and got us to thinking that we shouldn't look at Africa as these are black people we shouldn't deal with black people. I think Clinton has gotten Americans to look at this as opportunity. It doesn't matter what color people are – whether they're yellow, brown or whatever color they are – if there's opportunity. Opportunity is opportunity and that helps to heal the racial divide.
>
> I think the trade bill is a good start. It's not the full answer. It allows us to engage Africa in a real honest and open fashion.
>
> *Mel Foote*
> *President and CEO*
> *Constituency for Africa*
> *ACA Interview*

Finally, let me say that the legislation I sign today is about more than development and trade. It's about transforming our relationship with two regions full of good people trying to build good futures and who are very important to our own future. During the Cold War, to many Americans, Central America was a battleground and Africa was a backwater. All that has changed. We have worked hard the last few years to build genuine partnership with both regions — based on not what we can do for them, not what we can do about them, but on what we can do with them to build democracy together.

President William Jefferson Clinton
Signing of the Trade and Development Act of 2000
The White House, South Lawn
May 18, 2000

The African Growth and Opportunity Act (AGOA) will expand two-way trade and create incentives for the countries of sub-Saharan Africa to continue reforming their economies and increase their participation in the benefits of the global economy. President Clinton issued a proclamation on October 2, 2000, designating 34 countries in sub-Saharan Africa as eligible for AGOA's trade benefits..

The proclamation was the result of a public comment period and extensive interagency deliberations of each country's performance compared to the eligibility criteria established in the Act. The U.S. government will work with eligible countries to sustain their efforts to institute policy reforms and with the remaining 14 SSA countries to help them achieve eligibility.

This Act promises to deepen our economic partnership with Africa and expand two-way trade to the benefit of both partners. It will also encourage SSA countries to undertake economic reforms and to engage in the world economy.

President Clinton clenches his fists after signing the Trade and Development Act 2000 on the South Lawn at The White House. Standing next to Clinton is Chairman of the House Ways and Means Committee Rep. Bill Archer, R-Texas, Rep. Charles Rangel, D-NY, right, and behind the President is U.S. Trade Representative Charlene Barshefsky.

Photo Credit: Joe Marquette/AP

Provisions of the Act:

1. Establish, as U.S. policy, a framework of incentives to encourage greater economic growth and self-reliance through enhanced international trade and investment in Africa.

2. Expand the Generalized System of Preferences (GSP) program by providing duty-free treatment to virtually all products from sub-Saharan Africa. The GSP program provides preferential tariff treatment for imports of developing countries that satisfy certain eligibility requirements.

"In terms of President Clinton's support for the African Growth and Opportunity Act (AGOA), he never wavered. He always supported it. Initially, some members of his Administration publicly expressed skepticism, but for the most part there were some real workers who helped us gather votes. There were difficulties. There has been an anti-trade sentiment in Congress for some time now. Ironically, much of the support on this trade legislation came from Republicans instead of Democrats. The AGOA passed because Republicans voted for it not because of Democrats. He was able to work with people on both sides because otherwise he never would have gotten this passed. It shows a level of skill that I think sometimes goes unnoticed to be able to do that.

Gregory B. Simpkins
Vice President
The Foundation for
Democracy in Africa
Former Staff Member
House Africa Subcommittee
ACA Interview"

3. Extend duty-free, quota-free benefits to apparel made in Africa from U.S. yarn and U.S. fabric or from yarns not available in the United States.

4. Grant increasing duty-free, quota-free benefits to apparel made in Africa from African fabric. The escalating cap starts at 1.5 percent of U.S. imports of all apparels and rises over eight years to 3.5 percent. Africa's current share is only 1.1 percent of the U.S. apparel market.

5. Provide four years of special incentives for apparel industry investments in least developed countries.

6. Protect African workers and U.S. jobs by requiring tough safeguards against trans-shipment (i.e., shipping through a beneficiary country an item that was actually manufactured in a third country not eligible for the bill's preferential tariff treatment) and respect for internationally recognized worker rights and human rights.

7. Institutionalize annual high-level discussions to promote trade, investment and development through creation of a U.S.-Africa Trade and Economic Cooperation Forum.

8. Develop a plan to establish a free trade agreement with sub-Saharan African countries.

9. Provide additional technical assistance to help Africans take maximum advantage of the opportunities available in the expanding global trading system.

10. Encourage the American private sector to take a more active role in combating AIDS/HIV in Africa and establish eradication of

Photo Credit: Vince Lupo/AP

Rosa Whitaker, Assistant U.S. Trade Representative for Africa, poses in her Washington office.

AIDS as a top priority of the U.S. government. AGOA is the first trade bill to address the challenge of AIDS/HIV directly.

11.   Other provisions of the Act include: creation of an Overseas Private Investment Corporation (OPIC) Infrastructure Fund to encourage investment in crucial transportation, power, and other infrastructure projects; and expansion of trade financing through the U.S. Export-Import Bank.

The legislation, which is part of the Trade and Development Act of 2000, also includes the Caribbean Basin Trade Partnership Act, which offers temporary trade benefits to Caribbean Basin countries to facilitate their economic development and reconstruction after 1998´s devastating hurricanes and places them on a more equal competitive basis with Mexico in the U.S. market. Other legislative provisions include the development of trade and investment policies that facilitate the countries´ ultimate participation in the Free Trade Area of the Americas and trading rights the United States grants to other World Trade Organization members.

Photo Credit: Joe Marquette/AP

President Clinton speaks to the crowd on the South Lawn of the White House before signing the Trade and Development Act of 2000.

"At that moment (the signing of AGOA), we began a new relationship with sub-Saharan Africa. A relationship that is, at its foundation, based on the ideals of partnership and mutual respect. While not a panacea for all the ills plaguing sub Sahara, increased trade and investment have been proven vehicles for development in other regions of the world, providing essential capital through which struggling economies have increased their investment in their people.

I feel a sense of hope as we embark on this new journey. Hope that the prosperity that has touched every other major region of the world will now embrace Africa. Hope that the people of Africa will see the same potential in themselves that we, the United States, see in them. And, of course, hope that this legislation is the first step toward deeper ties between the United States and the nations of sub Saharan Africa.

Congressman Donald Payne
(D-NJ)
ACA Interview"

U.S.-South Africa Binational Commission

Founded under the leadership of President Clinton and President Mandela during the South African leader's state visit to Washington in October 1994, the U.S.-South Africa Binational Commission (BNC) was inaugurated on March 1, 1995. Co-chaired by Vice President Al Gore and South Africa President Thabo Mbeki, the BNC was created to promote a bilateral relationship between the United States and South Africa, to launch a new era in cooperation between the two countries by establishing permanent partnerships, to identi-

Vice President Al Gore conducting a meeting of the U.S.-South Africa Binational Commission in 1995. With him is Leon Fuerth, former U.S. Ambassador to South Africa Princeton Lyman, former Secretary of Commerce the late Ron Brown and Lauri Fitz Pegado, former Assistant Secretary and Director General U.S. Foreign Commercial Service.

fy U.S. expertise that can assist South Africa in meeting its Reconstruction and Development Program, and to build upon and expand involvement of private investors and non-government organizations.

Also known as the Gore-Mbeki Commission, the BNC has been meeting since 1994 and now comprises nine committees, including trade and investment, science and technology, sustainable energy, defense, and human resource development and education.

The BNC has been central to the process of renewing and strengthening cooperation in many areas. Under its auspices, the United States and Africa have worked to open markets, signed a trade and investment framework agreement, established a Trade and Investment Council, and negotiated a bilateral tax treaty and new pacts on civil aviation, extradition, and mutual legal assistance.

Led by U.S. Secretary of Agriculture Daniel Glickman, a delegation of U.S. Department of Agriculture (USDA) personnel participated in a February 1999 BNC meeting. Through the Agricultural Committee of the Commission, USDA implemented more than 15 technical assistance projects in South Africa, ranging from establishing financial systems in rural communities to providing formal educational opportunities for South African scientists to receive U.S. Masters and Doctoral degrees.

Through the BNC Environmental Management Working Group, the U.S. Environmental Protection Agency helps develop national and provincial environmental capacity. Activities include community-based solid waste management programs in targeted townships, support for community-based environmental organizations, environmental impact assessment and environmental management training for the mining sector, and increased access to environmental information.

Several other agencies, including the U.S. Departments of Transportation and Labor, are also active members of BNC committees.

We value our solid friendship with this great nation and consider it one of the pillars of our policy. President Clinton has been playing an active and very effective role. Under his leadership, the American contribution to the cause of peace has reached a new high. His continued involvement is appreciated by those of us who are committed to peace in the region.

President Hosni Mubarak
Press Conference with
President Clinton
Presidential Hall
The White House
July 1, 1999

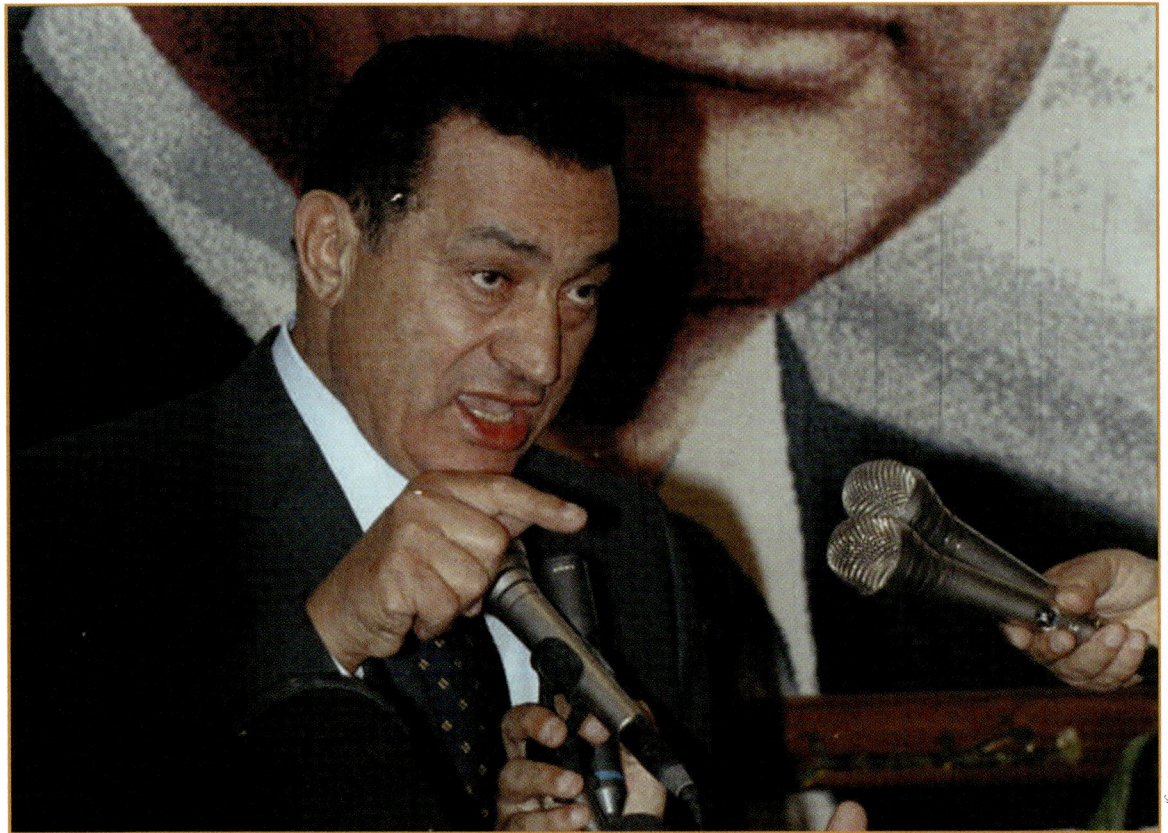

Photo Credit: Mohamed El-Dakhakhny/AP

Egyptian President Hosni Mubarak is seen in Cairo.

U.S.-Egyptian Partnership for Economic Growth and Development

The U.S.-Egyptian Partnership for Economic Growth and Development was announced by President Clinton and Egyptian President Hosni Mubarak in September 1994. The Partnership operates primarily through four subcommittees that direct public-private sector projects aimed at expanding economic growth and job opportunities in Egypt and at building mutually beneficial economic and commercial ties between the two countries. Co-chaired by Egyptian President Hosni Mubarak and U.S. Vice President Albert Gore, the initiative is also known as the Mubarak-Gore Partnership.

Partnership subcommittees are Economic Policy, Trade, Investment, and External Finance, Sustainable Development and the Environment, Technology, and Education and Human Resource Development. The Partnership also includes a Presidents' Council with 15 Egyptian and 15 American members who provide advice and counsel to both governments on private sector views of economic policy priorities to enhance commercial ties between the two countries. One-third of the Council's members changes every two years. U.S. members volunteer through the Department of Commerce, and Egyptian members are selected by the President.

Egyptian President Hosni Mubarak and Vice President Al Gore meet at the Blair House in Washington. The U.S.-Egyptian Partnership is co-chaired by Vice President Gore and President Mubarak.

The President's legacy to Africa will be Ron Brown. At Ron Brown's funeral, the President said he would not be President if it were not for Ron Brown. It takes a confident man to come from Arkansas and say that one black man is responsible for him becoming President of the United States and leader of the free world.

I wish we could keep it (Africa) on the radar screen because it's the right and moral thing to do. As the wealthiest and the most advanced industrialized country, it's going to be on the screen because the world has shrunk to such an extent that high technology is going to allow us to speedily invest and get a higher return on our investments.

America, in order to maintain its superior role in trade, will always have to develop new markets. And, unfortunately, the underdeveloped markets of Africa are where we have to go and where we will be going. Each and every day hundreds of transactions that we had not even thought of a decade ago are taking place today.

As with the stock market, when you find the returns being as high as they are, when you find stability, when you find democracy finally returning to Nigeria, all of these are good signs for investors. The more people that invest and the more people that come together and the more stability you find and the more jobs you have, the more peaceful people are in resolving their disputes.

Congressman
Charles B. Rangel (D-NY)
ACA Interview

President Thabo Mbeki with the former Secretary of Commerce, the late Ronald H. Brown.

The Ronald H. Brown Commercial Center

He was a bold thinker, a brilliant strategist, a devoted public servant, a good father and husband, and he was a terrific friend. I miss him terribly at this moment. But I cannot imagine a more fitting tribute to a man who proved that the Commerce Department could be an engine of growth and opportunity at home and abroad — who accepted my challenge to take a moribund agency and put it at the center of our economic policy, of our foreign policy, and of America's future in the world. He did his job well. I hope that when we leave here, we can do our job just as well so that this center will be a fitting, lasting legacy.

President William Jefferson Clinton
Opening of the Ronald H. Brown Commercial Center
March 28, 1998

President Clinton credits late Secretary of Commerce Ron Brown not only for his election but also for encouraging him to visit Africa. Dedicated by President Clinton in Johannesburg, South Africa,

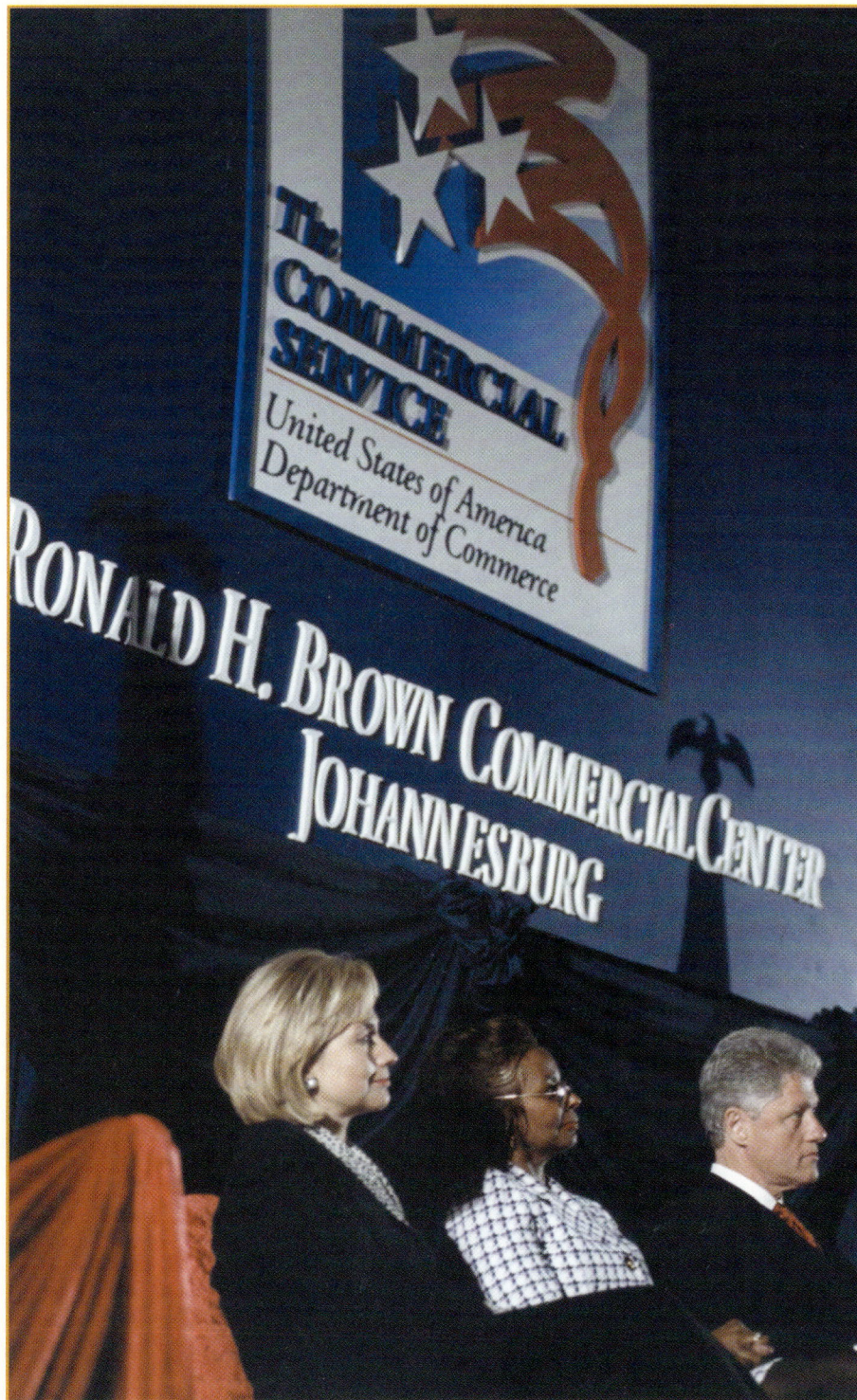

Photo Credit: Barbara Kinney/The White House

President Clinton, First Lady Hillary Rodham Clinton, and Alma Brown attend the dedication of the Ronald H. Brown Commercial Center in Johannesburg, South Africa.

on March 28, 1998, the Ronald H. Brown Commercial Center is a testament to Mr. Brown's foresight and commitment to creating an environment on the continent where businesses and, ultimately, the people of Africa can grow and thrive.

Operated and funded by the U.S. Department of Commerce, the Center is one of only four Centers worldwide. The Center will provide support for American companies looking to enter or expand into the Sub-Saharan African market. It will promote export through a range of support programs.

The Center also serves as a base for other agencies, such as the Export-Import Bank, the Trade Development Agency and the U.S. Trade Representative, to expand their assistance to business. The Center is staffed by three Foreign Commercial Service officers, an American administrator and 17 local staff. An Internet-linked commercial information resource center is staffed to answer trade-related queries from U.S. and African businesses and serves as a repository for economic and commercial reports from State Department officers stationed throughout Africa.

Photo Credit: Greg Gibson/AP

U.S. President Bill Clinton reacts as the ribbon cutting gets underway to open the Ronald H. Brown Commercial Center in Johannesburg, named after the U.S. Secretary of Commerce who died in a plane crash in the Balkans. Others are, from left to right, Alexis Herman, U.S. Secretary of Labor, First Lady Hillary Rodham Clinton and the widow of Ronald H. Brown, Alma Brown.

Safe Skies for Africa Initiative

In Senegal, President Clinton launched the Safe Skies for Africa Initiative (SSAI). This Presidential Initiative is designed to promote sustainable improvements in aviation safety and security in Africa by creating an environment to foster the growth of U.S.-Africa aviation services. Under the leadership of U.S. Secretary of Transportation Rodney Slater, the U.S. government acts as a technical advisor and facilitator of actions to be taken by African countries in partnership with the private sector, regional institutions and international civil aviation organizations.

The U.S. government will fund aviation safety and security surveys. Nine African countries have been selected to participate in this Initiative -- Angola, Cameroon, Cape Verde, Côte d'Ivoire, Kenya, Mali, Tanzania, Zimbabwe, and Namibia.

The goals of SSAI are to quadruple the number of sub-Saharan African countries that meet International Civil Aviation Organization safety standards, to improve security at eight to 12 airports within the region in three years, and to improve regional air navigation services.

As a result of this Initiative, U.S. air services are already improving, Secretary Slater told the House Transportation and Infrastructure Subcommittee on Aviation. "…after Ethiopia was found to meet ICAO standards, Ethiopian Airlines began direct service between Addis Ababa and Washington's Dulles Airport, becoming the fourth Sub Saharan Africa airline in addition to South African Airways, Ghana Airways and Air Afrique – to serve the United States. U.S. carriers also are showing a greater interest in serving Africa, with Polar Air Cargo recently being authorized to fly between New York and South Africa, Zimbabwe and Kenya."

"Today, fully one-half of all international commerce is conducted by air – but you can't trade if you can't get there. Furthermore, tourism, the world's largest industry, is rapidly becoming one of the most important and lucrative businesses on the continent, and the development of the tourism sector is high priority for many African governments. Recognizing that, the African leaders with whom I have met have fully embraced the Safe Skies for Africa initiative as a vehicle to provide for aviation safety and airport security.

As a result of the initiative, U.S.-Africa air services are already improving. Last month, after Ethiopia was found to meet ICAO standards, Ethiopian Airlines began direct service between Addis Ababa and Washington's Dulles Airport, becoming the fourth sub-Saharan African airline – in addition to South African Airways, Ghana Airways and Air Afrique – to serve the United States. U.S. carriers also are showing a greater interest in serving Africa, with Polar Air Cargo recently being authorized to fly between New York and South Africa, Zimbabwe, and Kenya.

Rodney Slater
Secretary of the U.S.
Department of Transportation
Testimony before the House
Transportation and
Infrastructure
Subcommittee on Aviation
July 30, 1998

President Clinton embraces Transportation Secretary Rodney Slater during a news conference in the Old Executive Office Building in Washington.

Debt Relief

Already, debt relief is making a difference around the world. Mozambique, for example, is buying much-needed medicines for government clinics. Uganda used its savings to double its primary school enroll-ment. By lifting the weakest, poorest among us, we lift all the rest of us, as well. I hope that this idea will be a priority in our foreign policy for a long time to come, no less important than promoting trade, investment and financial stability. It will be good for our economy, because it represents an investment in future markets, good for our security because in the long run it is dangerously destabiliz-ing to have half the world on the cutting edge of technology while the other half struggles on the bare edge of survival.

President William Jefferson Clinton
Funding For Debt Relief
The White House, East Room
November 6, 2000

President Clinton spearheaded an international effort to bail out debt-laden Third World countries on the theory that it would relieve them of interest payments that might other-wise go for education and other initiatives to help their economies. In October 2000, Congress passed legislation that is part of a major foreign aid package that will include the full $435 million sought by President Clinton for Third World debt relief language allowing the International Monetary Fund to release $800 million for additional debt forgiveness from the sale of its gold reserves.

Under the initiative, known as the enhanced Heavily Indebted Poor Country (HIPC) initiative, savings from debt relief will be directed to education, health care, AIDS prevention, and other critical needs in qualifying countries.

The debt relief will come in two parts: $435 million funneled through the World Bank to regional African and Latin American banks and the rest from legislative language authorizing the IMF to use the full proceeds from the sale of gold from its reserve to finance a new debt relief trust fund. The money is to be made available February 15, 2001.

For the average HIPC country, the share of scarce government revenue devoted to debt service (primarily interest payments) could fall by 25 percent to 50 percent, according to The White House. For example, Mozambique's debt is expected to be reduced by some $3.5 billion, which could cut in half the share of government revenues allocated to external debt service, and free about $96 million in budgetary resources each year. These savings are equivalent to double the 1998 health budget in a country where children are more than three times as likely to die before the age of five as they are to go to secondary school. In Uganda, enhanced debt reduc-tion could allow health and education spending to increase by 50 percent between 1998 and 2001, and rural development expenditures to more than double.

An unidentified young boy supports members of ActUp, a group fighting for the rights of the people living with AIDS, during a protest in Durban, South Africa.

President Clinton speaks at an event in the East Room of the White House after signing the Foreign Operations Appropriations Bill on November 6, 2000. The $435 million sought by President Clinton is for poor countries' debt relief.

President Clinton holds a two-day-old boy who was named Bill Clinton in honor of the President's visit to Wanyange Village in Uganda.

Strengthening
Human *and*
Infrastructure
Development

Africa is mankind's first home. We all came out of Africa. We must preserve the magnificent natural environment that is left. We must manage the water and forest. We must learn to live in harmony with other species. You must learn how to fight drought and famine and global warming. And we must share with you the technology that will enable you to preserve your environment and provide more economic opportunity to your people.

President William Jefferson Clinton
Remarks to the People of Ghana
March 23, 1998

President Clinton's Partnership for Economic Growth and Opportunity in Africa Initiative extends beyond the usual foreign aid programs to address education issues, the empowerment of women, health, agriculture, energy and the environment. While democracy and trade are important, President Clinton obviously believes the development of infrastructure and human capital must be addressed as well.

President Clinton has an uncanny ability to understand the tremendous confluence of issues, programs, and policies that affect people's lives. Unlike any American president before him, he sought information on the real issues, examined and explored them in more detail on both sides of the ocean, and decided to visit several African countries to see the beautiful land and its diverse people.

Addressing a confluence of U.S. government Africa policy issues soon caught on at several departments and agencies. Unlike any other time in America's history, the U.S. government is working across agencies to address agriculture, education, health, environmental, and energy issues. The end result has been more effective programs, stronger U.S.-Africa partnerships, and strategic short- and long-term planning.

It is no surprise that this would happen when a president refuses to embrace preconceived notions and past indifferences, is apologetic for past U.S. Africa policy failures, and forges ahead to build partnerships and implement programs and policies that benefit both the United States and Africa.

The Benin dancers are performing one of their ceremonial dances, demonstrating the diverse culture and beauty of Africa.

Education for Democracy and Development Initiative

At the request of Malian President Konare, President Clinton created the Education for Development and Democracy Initiative (EDDI) to strengthen educational systems and democratization principles and to fortify and extend vital development partnerships between the United States and Africa. EDDI programs are African-led and are primarily concentrated on improving the quality of and access to education, enhancing the availability of technology, and increasing citizen participation in government.

EDDI is centered around three principal strategies: community resource centers, public-private partnerships, and educating and empowering girls. Key components include: primary, secondary, and higher education; professional training; and civil education. EDDI seeks to establish up to 20 new university partnerships, 50 school-to-school linkups, and to implement a variety of girls' and women's leadership activities.

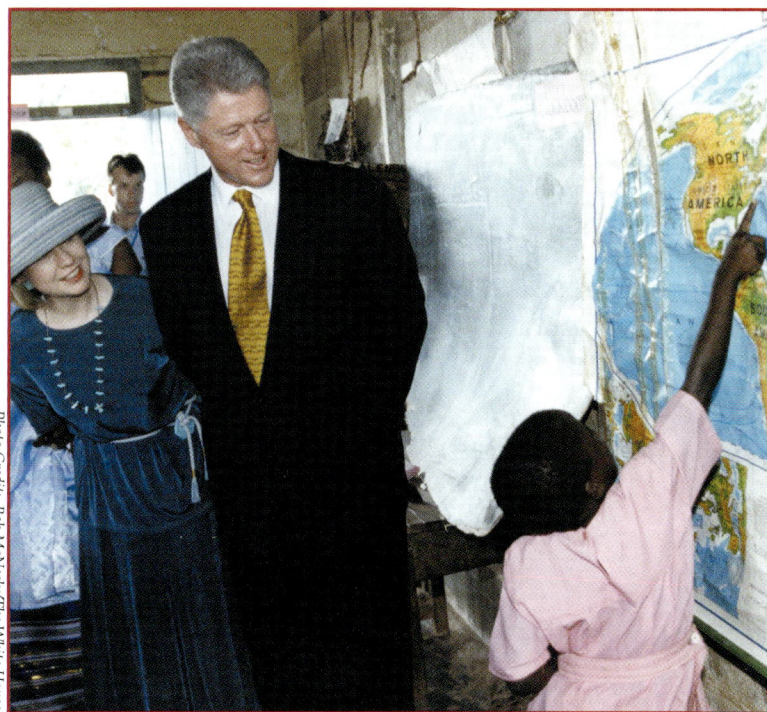

Photo Credit: Bob McNeely/The White House

The President and First Lady observe a class at the Kissowera School in Mukono, Uganda.

The program is coordinated by the U.S. Department of State, U.S. Agency for International Development, and the Peace Corps in consultation with African Education Ministers and U.S. and African private sector experts. The program includes seven countries – Ghana, Senegal, Mali, Uganda, Rwanda, Botswana, and South Africa.

Prior to President Clinton's visit, he met with President Alpha Oumar Konare of Mali and talked about ways to support Africa and how do we make more African countries consider and work around the issue of democracy. President Konare said to President Clinton the United States wants all of us to become countries of democracy but what can we do if our countries are poor, our people are going to bed hungry and uneducated? Having put that on President Clinton's mind, they talked about what kind of initiative could we do to uplift Africa. The initiative, Education for Development and Democracy Initiative, was created and launched at that time.

After President Clinton came back, he said we have got to do more. We've got to do more also to enhance women as we build this education issue. He's a president who has never worked alone. He has worked to include people. Another means that he thought about was technology. So one of the partnerships is technology partnerships. We have one that I'm so excited about, which is a partnership of what we call telemedicine, which has connected Howard University Hospital with the University off the Transky. When there is a difficulty surgery or delivery at the University of the Transky, there is a computer by that patient's bed where the doctor can type in the information and send it back to Howard University and get an immediate response from a doctor there. This is the kind of thing that President Clinton has moved forward within this initiative.

Dr. Sarah E. Moten
Coordinator
Education for Development
and Democracy Initiative
U.S. Agency for International
Development
ACA Interview

Africa Food Security Initiative

In March 1998, President Clinton announced the creation of the Africa Food Security Initiative (AFSI) to assist African nations in strengthening and protecting agriculture and food security in a number of key areas, including:

- healthy and alternative crop production;
- better market efficiency and distribution of existing crops;
- increased trade and investment in agricultural industries;
- attacking crop diseases; and
- increasing access to modern agricultural technology systems to assist with increased crop production and distribution.

AFSI is currently active in Mali, Ethiopia, Mozambique, Malawi, and Uganda, and will be expanded to include Liberia, Rwanda, and Zimbabwe. USAID's goal for this program over the 10-year period is to improve child survival rates by increasing access to food and essential health services as a means to protect Africa's most vulnerable.

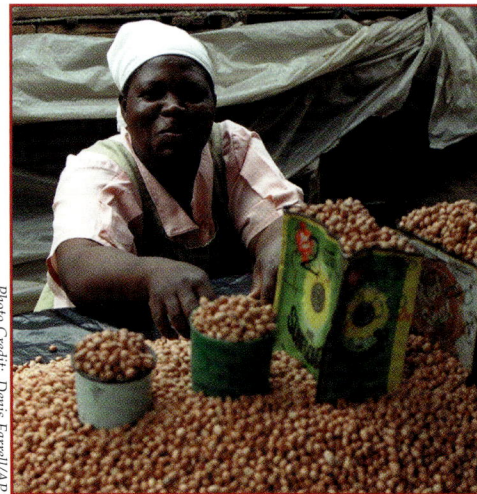

Photo Credit: Denis Farrell/AP

In June 1998, President Clinton also announced a wheat donation "Food Aid Initiative," which authorizes proceeds from the sale of 203 metric tons of wheat and wheat products to assist agricultural development projects and local business initiatives in Kenya, Côte d' Ivoire, Equatorial Guinea, Togo, Zimbabwe, South Africa, Benin, Angola, Swaziland, and Tanzania.

A woman sells ground nuts at an informal market in Harare, Zimbabwe.

Empowering Women

In Senegal, President Clinton was introduced to a group of villagers who agreed to stop the practice of female genital mutilation (FGM). In March 1999, Senegal passed legislation banning the practice. This historic development will affect approximately one-third of Senegal's female youth destined to submit to this procedure as a rite of passage into womanhood. By making this dangerous practice illegal, the law provides political and legal legitimacy to the women and men who are working toward consensual banning of the practice locally.

Tostan, USAID/UNICEF-financed Senegalese non governmental organization, is directly responsible for this bold move by the Senegalese government. The law was proposed

Nigerian women and children pose at the National Center for Women Development in Abuja during President Clinton's visit. Female genital mutilation is an issue that is being discussed in Nigeria as well.

Prominent African businesswomen at the African Business Roundtable Annual General Meeting in Casablanca, Morocco. These women, from the public and private sector, presented position papers on fostering the empowerment of women.

to the Senegalese Cabinet through a petition signed by Tostan-trained women.

Acting to further empower African women, USAID also provided the Ghanaian Association of Women Entrepreneurs (GAWE) with computers and equipment necessary to connect it to a nationwide Internet network. Powernet, an informal electronic conference system still in the design stage, will enable elected female officials and other leading women from across Africa to interact with each other and with their counter parts in the United States.

Photo Credit: Arse Kassagne

Prominent lawyer, Marie-Elyse Gbedo is Vice Chairperson of the Association of Women Lawyers in Benin, West Africa.

A group of 20 women from Africa participated in a program entitled, "African Women: An Emerging Economic Force," sponsored by the Department of State's Office of International Visitors. The program examined how women work individually through networking to promote economic activity and private enterprise. The group traveled from Washington, D.C., to Pittsburgh, Denver, Chicago and Kansas City, where they discussed a wide array of issues, including gender equality, shaping national policy, entrepreneurship and non-traditional careers.

✛

"It was undoubtedly the fall of the Berlin Wall that paved the way for President Clinton to consider Africa, no longer as a means to develop a certain strategy aiming at preserving U.S. political interests vis-à-vis Russia, but rather a partner who deserves respect and durable development, in spite of the wars, famine and corruption.

It's undeniable that Bill Clinton, thanks to a sincere desire to better know Africa and make Africa known to his fellow Americans, has opened the way for a cooperation based on mutual respect between American and African partners.

Bill Clinton's departure will not stop the process. The dialogue will continue in order to follow up on the President's efforts to boost relations.

Marie-Elyse Gbedo
Vice Chairperson
Association of Women
Lawyers
Benin, West Africa

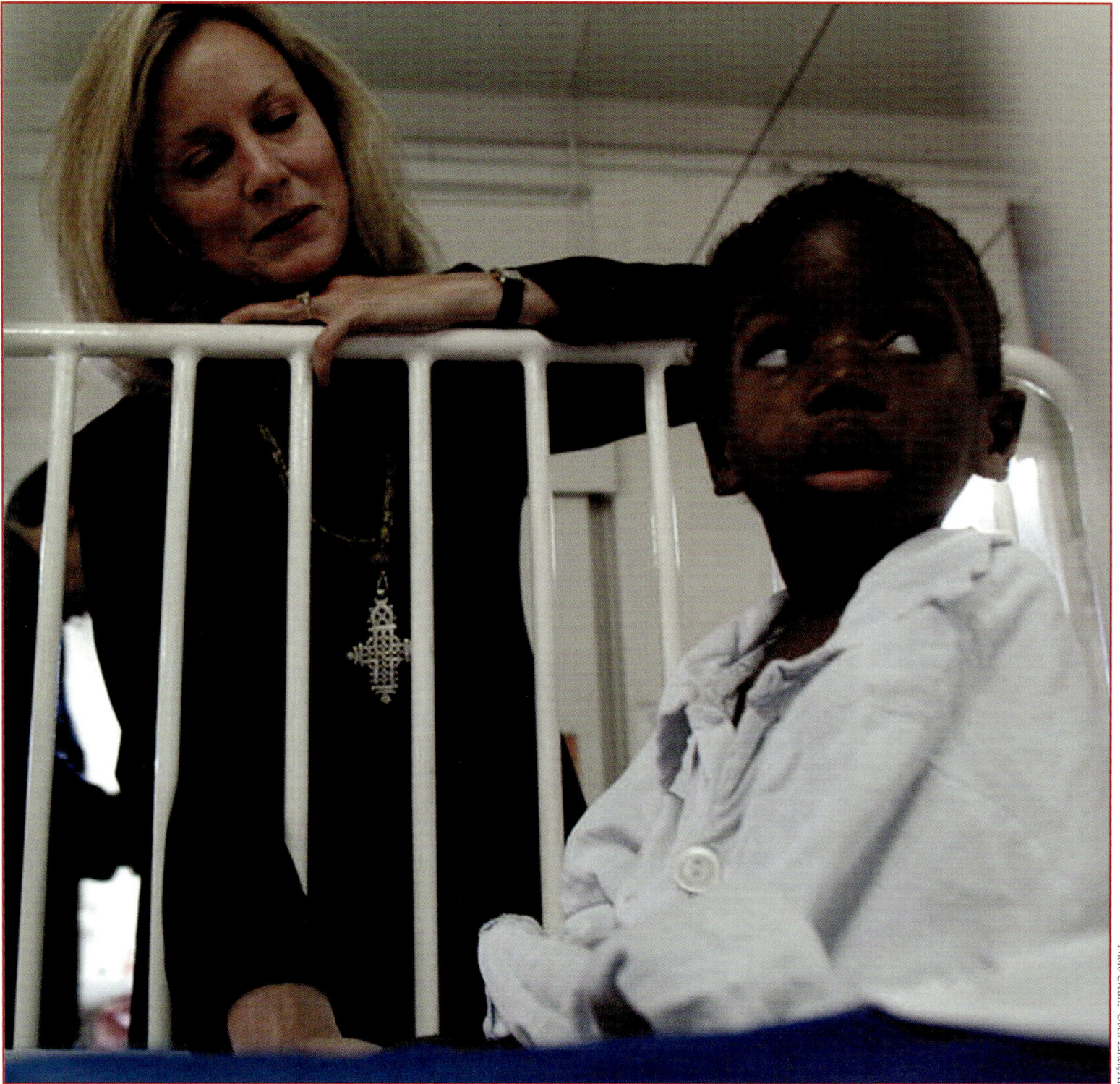

U.S. White House AIDS Czar Sandra Thurman with an HIV positive child at King Edward's Hospital in Durban, South Africa.

HIV/AIDS

On May 10, 2000, President Clinton issued an executive order that increases Africans' access to HIV/AIDs pharmaceuticals and medical technologies. The executive order will allow African countries to produce or obtain drugs for countering AIDs that are cheaper than those patented in the United States. President Clinton took this historic step after House and Senate negotiators dropped a similar provision from the African Growth and Opportunity Act.

The EO further states that the United States shall encourage all beneficiary Sub-Saharan African countries to implement policies designed to address the underlying causes of the HIV/AIDS crisis by, among other things, encouraging practices that will prevent further transmission and infection, stimulating development of the infrastructure necessary to deliver adequate health services, and encouraging policies that provide an incentive for public and private research on, and development of, vaccines and other medical innovations to combat the HIV/AIDs epidemic in Africa.

While visiting the National Center for Women Development in Abuja, Nigeria, President Clinton announced more than $20 million to support President Obasanjo's aggressive campaigns against malaria, polio and HIV/AIDS, and recognized President Obasanjo's extraordinary efforts to mobilize other African leaders in these battles. President Clinton and President Obasanjo pledged to join forces to fight HIV/AIDS and other devastating diseases.

Joined by youth groups, people living with AIDS, religious and business leaders, unions, women's groups, and the military, Presidents Clinton and Obasanjo reinforced the need for leadership, resources and action by all segments of society to combat HIV/AIDS. The two leaders highlighted and praised the efforts of Nigeria's non-governmental organizations, including the Society of Women Against AIDS in Nigeria, the Muslim Sisters Organization and the Nigerian Network of People Living with AIDS.

Two visits in the Spring of 1999 by the director of the White House Office of National AIDS Policy, Sandra Thurman, to study issues involving AIDS-affected children and orphans are direct outcomes of President's 1998 trip. After Deputy President Thabo Mbeki's October 1998 pronouncement of the Partnership Against AIDS program, Vice President Gore sent a supportive letter. USAID is also actively supporting several HIV/AIDS initiatives on the continent.

President Clinton greets HIV-positive AIDS Activist Sean Sasser during the first White House Conference on AIDS. Health Secretary Donna Shalala is at right. AIDS has been a priority for President Clinton in the United States as well as Africa.

President Clinton signs the World AIDS Day Proclamation as Director of AIDS Policy Sandy Thurman looks on.

President Clinton and former U.N. Ambassador Dr. Andrew Young talk during opening ceremonies of the National Summit on Africa on February 17, 2000 in Washington.

The *Sustainers* *of the* Legacy

A multitude of Africans, African Americans, and Americans, in general, have labored tirelessly for years to improve U.S.-Africa relations, often walking the halls of Congress and frequently requesting White House involvement. All of this was to no avail until the election of President Clinton.

Too often, it appeared the legislative struggle would last a lifetime and no one, with the exception of the Congressional Black Caucus and a few other members of Congress would consider pursuing serious U.S.-Africa policy. However, Africare, TransAfrica, Constituency for Africa, the African American Institute, and a number of other organizations and individuals continued to fight, march, inform, and educate whenever and wherever there was an opportunity to do so.

Sadly, many Americans know very little about the work of these organizations because the media too often either did not cover Africa at all or only focused on Africa's poverty, famine, genocide, and war. Now that President Clinton has helped to broaden the camera lens on Africa, the media have an opportunity through these organizations to help inform the American populace about Africa, "the cradle of civilization."

Friends of Africa

Photo Credits: Ed Betz/AP

Reverend Leon Sullivan and Coretta Scott King address passengers at John F. Kennedy International Airport before boarding a flight to Accra, Ghana, where they led the United States delegation to the Fifth African-African American Summit, sponsored by the International Foundation for Education and Self-Help (IFESH).

Boxing great Muhammad Ali, flanked by actress Angela Bassett, and
TransAfrica President Randall Robinson spars, for photographers.

Bart O. Nnaji, chairman of the Nigerian Peoples Forum, with
Dr. Erieka Bennett.

With entertainer Stevie Wonder standing by, actor Morgan Freeman shakes hands with South African President Thabo Mbeki as
President Clinton looks on.

What sets Clinton apart from the presidents before him and perhaps even those who are in the political fray today is that he feels comfortable among all peoples, including people of African descent. He has no pretenses about his interactions -- his interactions and his bearing are genuinely presidential. One can say that if his relationships with people of African descent are a pretense, then more leaders should pretend like that, for in the end the outcome is better for everyone and the world is a better place. Mr. Clinton has appointed people of African descent to very important cabinet positions.

For sure, he was not the first to appoint African-Americans to cabinet positions but he genuinely empowered those he appointed in those positions. For example, the late Ron Brown came to his position of Secretary of Commerce after serving as the Chairman of the Democratic National Committee -- a position which in so many ways can dictate success or failure of a candidate running for the presidency. To have trusted Mr. Brown with such defining responsibility speaks volumes about Clinton's belief that an African-American can make a significant contribution to the future of America.

Bart O. Nnaji
Chairman,
Nigerian Peoples Forum
ALCOA Foundation Chair
Professor in Engineering
University of Pittsburgh

Congressional Black Caucus Chairwoman Representative Maxine Waters, D-CA, laughs as Bill Cosby mugs for the camera during a ceremony where members of the Caucus were sworn in. Cosby was a featured speaker.

American civil rights advocate and Presidential Special Envoy to Africa Reverend Jesse Jackson is greeted by a line of Senegalese women on Goree Island.

Photo Credits: J. Scott Applewhite/AP

Detroit Mayor Dennis Archer (second left) was a member of the official delegation accompanying President Clinton to Nigeria last August.

Mr. & Mrs. Noah Samara. Mr. Samara is President of Worldspace Corporation, which is bringing digital radio technology to Africa.

Photo Credits: Courtesy of ACA

"

President Clinton began a legacy of America dealing with Africa on a one-on-one basis. He established a relationship with Africa that placed Africa on the type of playing field that was not so different from the United States' relationship with Asia, or the United States' relationship with Latin America. That was a clear watershed in American politics.

I believe that trade and economic development is one of the areas where President Clinton should be most proud of the achievements of his Administration. Under his leadership, the Congress passed historic trade legislation that marked the beginning of a positive era in US relations with sub- Saharan Africa. Until earlier this year, Africa was the only region in the world with which the US did not have a comprehensive, trade and investment bilateral relationship. Of course, that changed under Clinton's leadership. That just opens up quite a large area of possibilities for U.S. businesses wanting to do business in Africa.

Seeing President Clinton in Africa both times, especially wearing African traditional clothing, was psychologically one of the most endearing things that a President of the United States could have done. These things may look to many as largely symbolic, but these are like watershed things that no other President has done. He visited Africa to empathize with the plight of the continent and the potential of the continent. All were captured in the way he approached the continent physically and from a policy point of view; and his going back a second time was absolutely great.

Noah Samara
President
Worldspace Corporation
ACA Interview

Comedian Dick Gregory, left; former Washington, D.C., Mayor Marion Barry; Reverend Leon Sullivan, second from right; and former mayor of New York City David Dinkins, right, arrive at the Regina Mundi Catholic Church in Soweto, South Africa. Rev. Sullivan is founder of the International Foundation for Education and Self-Help, the sponsor of the Summit.

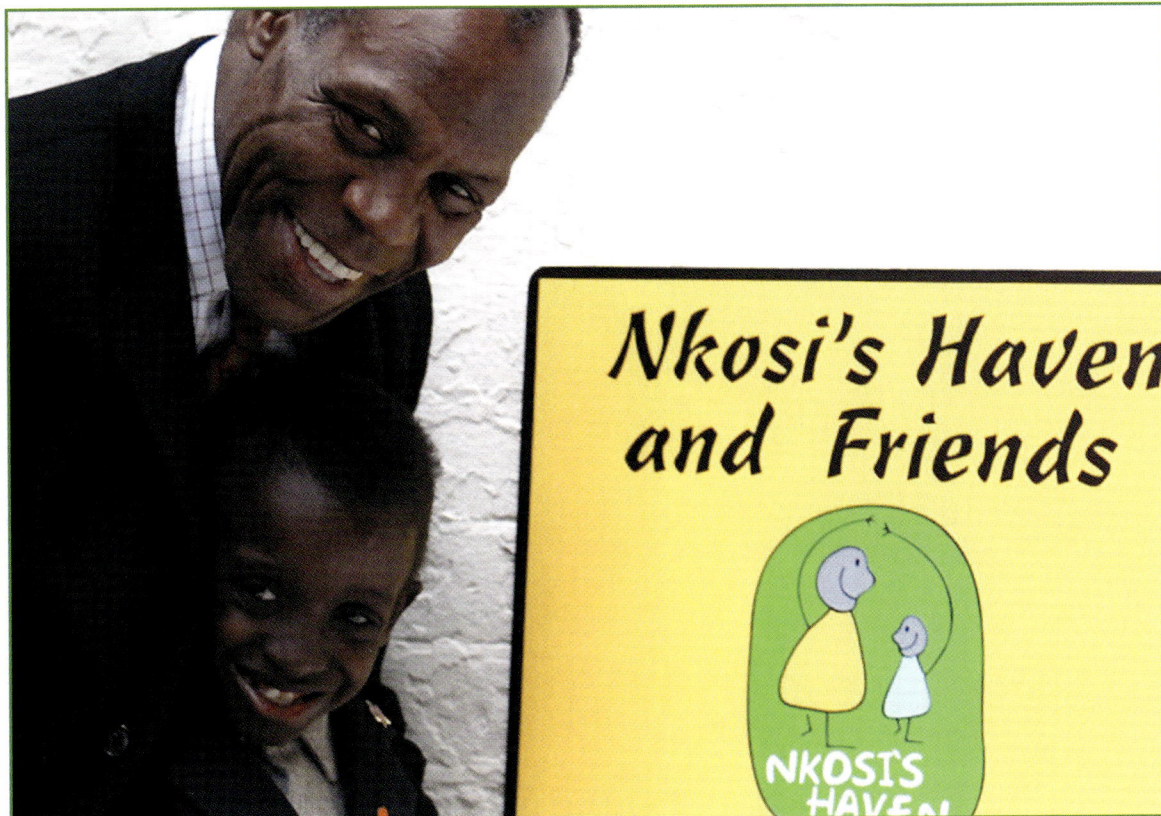

Actor and U.N. Development Program Global Goodwill Ambassador Danny Glover hugs Nkosi Johnson, an 11-year-old boy infected with HIV, in Johannesburg, South Africa.

Jabrawn Bennett and Jonard Bennett are fans of President Clinton

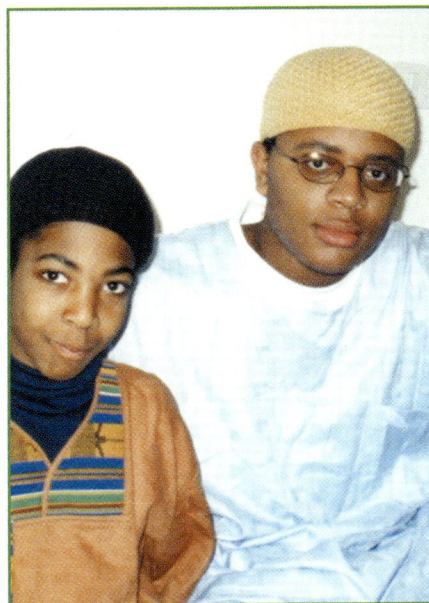

Two fans of President Clinton, Mahar Alexander Bennington Cooke and Aharone Ben Israel. Cooke, will be studying in South Africa.

My mother is from the Bronx and my father is from Namibia. Namibia gained its Independence in 1990 and we picked up and moved back to Africa. That definitely was a turning point in my life. Initially, it was not a happy time in my life, but became a life defining experience and one of the best experiences of my life because it finally gave me an opportunity to explore a side of me which had been a mystery to me up to that point. I found out I am very much African. Although I had traveled to Africa, I had never lived in a country I could call my own. It was a wonderful experience and still is today.

President Clinton is seen as the most progressive President that we've seen. As a black person, it was obvious that here was a President who sincerely cared about what was going on in the Continent of Africa.

There was something interesting that I heard in the debates between George Bush and Al Gore. The question was asked what his agenda would be in terms of foreign policy. He (George Bush) named the Far East, Europe, and he didn't name Africa. And he wasn't ashamed. It was supporting my belief there is just a general apathy about Africa. Africa needs America to play a role in its development.

Whether Americans like it or not, the U.S. is a world leader in terms of economic development and will play a huge role in Africa's development. Africa has its own role in its development, but I hope the incoming Administration has Africa on its agenda.

Dantago Gurirab
Graduate of Morehouse College
Bronx, NY

Photo Credits: Denis Farrell/AP

The Honorable Minister Louis Farrakhan, left, leader of the Nation of Islam, with Winnie Mandela at a news conference in Soweto, South Africa.

Photo Credit: Courtesy of ACA

Dr. Dorothy Height, president emeritus of the National Council of Negro Women and U.S. Secretary of Labor Alexis Herman, left.

Photo Credit: Courtesy of ACA

H.E. Ruth Perry former Head of State, Liberia, right, with Dr. Smith, president of NCNW at Dr. Height's Birthday Tribute.

ACA Board Member Samuel Dossou poses with Winnie Mandela.

Photo Credit: Courtesy of ACA

President Clinton greets Dr. Niara Sudarkasa, former President of Lincoln University. Dr. Sudarkasa traveled with President Clinton to several African countries.

Photo Courtesy of ACA

Lota Mushaw, President of Lam & Associates, with Prince Asiel, International Ambassador of the Hebrew Israelites, and Sister Claudette Muhammad, Chief of Protocol to the Honorable Minister Louis Farrakhan.

Photo Credit: Courtesy of ACA

"It is really Bill Clinton who has put Africa back on the map geo-politically. He has put it on the minds of the world from an international point of view. And (he) has really given leadership in that Africa is not third world, third rate or third issue as it relates to the Clinton Administration. I think we have to be historically correct and politically correct by saying it was Bill Clinton who was sensitized by the Africans within his Administration so that Africa would be an important agenda item.

I don't think that this door can ever be closed again by any Administration. I don't think this Genie can be put back into the bottle. African Americans will not be trivialized for talking about Africa now and Africans will not be relegated as a footnote of the Clinton Administration's foreign policy. We are prepared -- meaning those who have lived in Africa and those who understand the importance of Africa -- and are recommitted to making sure that the legacy that President Clinton started is constant and before anybody who takes that office from here to eternity that Africa and Africans in America will be a factor to deal with in this international arena."

Prince Asiel
International Ambassador
African Hebrew Israelites

93

Former Washington Mayor Marion Barry, center, and his wife, Cora Masters Barry, left, look on as poet Maya Angelou speaks at the MCI Center in Washington, DC in October 1998.

Rep. Jesse Jackson, Jr. (D-Ill), left, and his father Rev. Jesse Jackson answer questions from reporters at The National Press Club on February 1, 1996.

Former New York Mayor David Dinkins, center, marches at the front of the 29th Annual African American Day parade in Harlem flanked by Al Sharpton, left, and Ruth Messinger in September 1997.

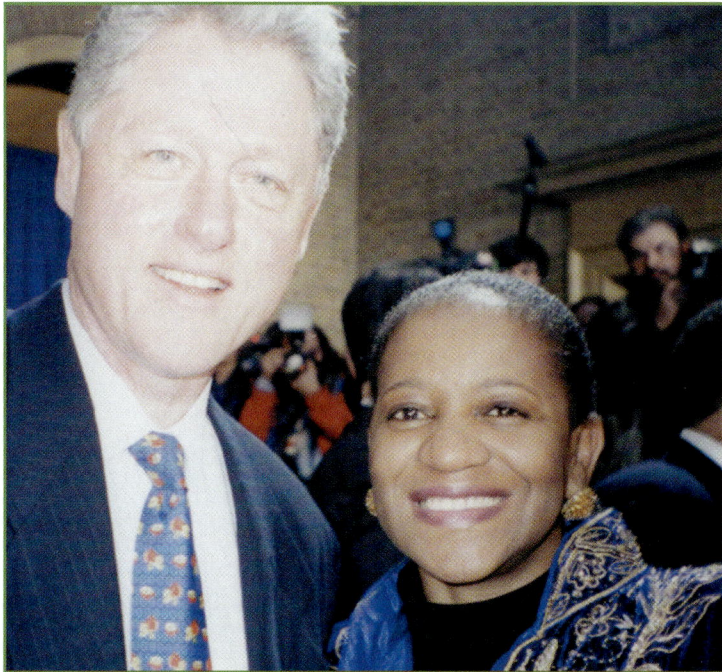

President Clinton and Dr. Erieka Bennett.

Historian and Chairman of the Initiative for One America with President and Mrs. Clinton.

President Clinton poses with Sharolyn Rosier Hyson, President of Integrated Communications Solutions, Inc., and her parents, James and Vivian Rosier. Mrs. Rosier Hyson is a former White House Editor.

Coretta Scott King, center, widow of slain civil rights leader Dr. Martin L. King, Jr., talks to reporters outside the Justice Department on April 8, 1998, after meeting with Attorney General Janet Reno about the 1968 assassination of her husband. She is flanked by former U.N. Ambassador Andrew Young; her son, Dexter; her daughter, The Rev. Bernice King; and Walter Fauntroy, former Congressional Delegate for the District of Columbia.

Rep. Harold Ford, Jr. (D-Tenn), poses on Capitol Hill in Washington, D.C., on March 22, 2000. The two-term Memphis Democrat is the youngest member of Congress. He succeeds his father Harold Ford, Sr., who spent 22 years as Tennessee's first black congressman.

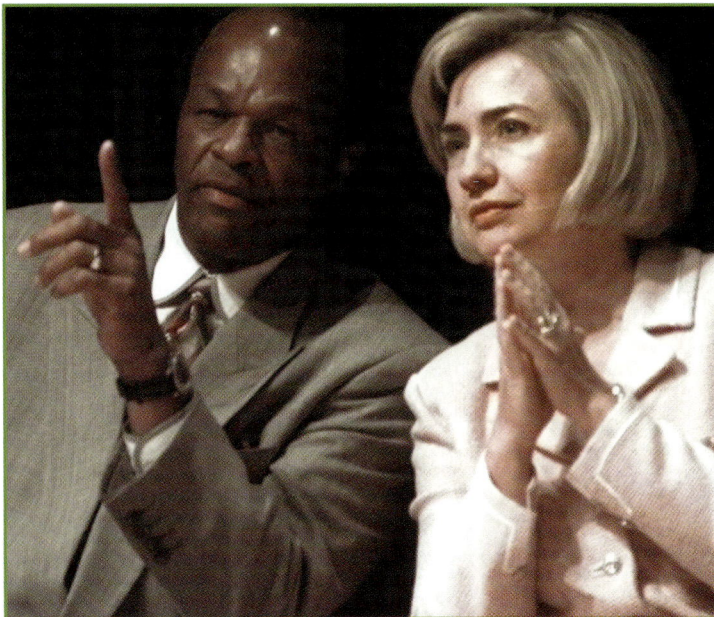

First Lady Hillary Rodham Clinton and former Washington Mayor Marion Barry talk during a meeting of the Youth Leadership Institute in Washington on July 30, 1997.

President Clinton is applauded by former Congressman Louis Stokes, left, Secretary of Transportation Rodney Slater, right, Sen. Mike DeWine (R-OH), and former Sen. Carol Moseley Braun, after signing the Underground Railroad Act in the Oval Office at The White House on July 21, 1998. Sen. Moseley Braun and Reps. Stokes and DeWine were sponsors of the legislation, which authorizes the National Park Service to spend $500,000 annually to link the sites of the Underground Railroad, produce educational materials, and enter partnerships to commemorate the 19th century escape route.

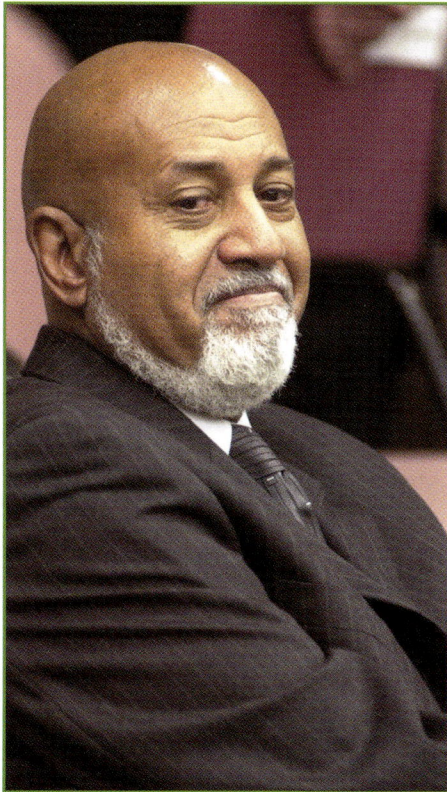

Representative Alcee Hastings (D- FL) watches the manual count of absentee ballots at the Broward County Courthouse in Ft. Lauderdale, Florida, in November 2000.

Tipper Gore, wife of Vice President Al Gore, speaks to Lottie Shackelford, former Little Rock, Arkansas, mayor, and Terrence Roberts, one of the black students who integrated Little Rock Central High in 1957, after a Gore-Lieberman rally during the 2000 presidential campaign.

Anita Omitowoju, President of Moremi Marketing, is a marketing and public relations consultant.

U.S. Secretary of Transportation Rodney Slater and Nardos Bekele-Thomas, Senior Private Sector Policy Advisor, Africa Bureau, United Nations.

President Clinton has made a significant change in the perception of development strategy in Africa. Especially, where there was skepticism about trade and investment. He introduced to Africa the concept that aid should be a mutually beneficial instrument and tool. That helped my work in private sector development because what we would like to inculcate in the minds of Africa and Africans is the fact that aid is just being dependent. It teaches how to receive. It's not helping the productive capacity of the continent.

There are so many things the new Administration can do. First of all, it has to build on what President Clinton has started. In promoting trade and investment, there are certain things that need to be learned. Africans should learn how to run businesses, africans should also have access to capital. There should also be technology transfer in order for real trade to take place.

Nardos Bekele-Thomas
Senior Private
Sector Policy Advisor
Africa Bureau
United Nations
ACA Interview

John H. Johnson, Chief Executive Officer of Johnson Publishing, receives a Presidential Medal of Freedom from President Clinton. Johnson Publishing also produces Ebony South Africa.

Dr. Erieka Bennett with World Bank Africa Club Officers, Thelma Jones, Sidi Jammeh, and Eric Chinje, during the press conference announcing the first Africa Day at The World Bank.

"President Clinton is so loved and respected, some Africans jokingly talk about forming a United States of Africa and making him President."

Reverend Victoria Ogun

ACA staffer, Reverend Victoria Ogun, standing with Paul Caldwell, former chairman of Exxon-Mobil, Nigeria, at a Friends of Nigeria Dinner, sponsored by Exxon-Mobil Nigeria.

Dr. Yacouba Fassassi, Special Advisor to the President of Benin

> In a post-Cold War era when interest in Africa is at its lowest, President Clinton's trip to West, Central, East and Southern Africa in 1998 and 2000 helped millions of Americans discover the real Africa, a continent facing many challenges, but also a land of hardworking, courageous people such as those in our small West African nation of Benin. The negative image of Africa in the United States is, to a large extent, the result of the lack of knowledge about Africa on the part of most Americans.
>
> President Clinton's trips during which Africa was on the evening news on TV and on the radio, as well as newspaper headlines, introduced Africa to the American public who knew nothing or very little about our continent which the American media pervasively portray in a negative light.
>
> It is not a secret, President Clinton has been the most popular U.S. president among Black Americans. This popularity, clearly, enhances our appreciation for the president as we, the government of Benin, are engaged in a sincere reconciliation process with our brothers and sisters in the diaspora.
>
> ***Dr. Yacouba Fassassi***
> ***Special Advisor to the***
> ***President of Benin, General***
> ***Matheiu Kerekou***
> ***Chairman of the Council of***
> ***Economic Advisors for***
> ***Republic of Benin***

Seeing how today's society is going down hill. I think it is very important that teenagers pay close attention to politics so our children and grandchildren will have a better future. I have to be honest and say that I really haven't paid much attention to politics. However, I do know that the Honorable William Jefferson Clinton really has made an impact while serving both of his terms. The former President may not know this, but he has made a lasting impression on today's society of teenagers as well as African Americans.

President Clinton's legacy to Africa has shown that he has concerns for African-Americans, not only in the United States, but in other countries as well. He is also setting examples as to making peace with leaders of other countries. This is showing younger generations that may not share the same interest as them.

I will truly miss President Clinton being the head of the White House and our mighty nation. He was one of the few Presidents that was considered "cool" to younger Americans. As a President, he will never be forgotten and his legacy will forever flourish in all African American's hearts.

Tiffany Mayo
Gwynn Park Senior
High School
Brandywine, Maryland
Known for the poem
she recited by at
the Million Man March
on October 16, 1995

I was happy to see President Clinton visit Africa twice. I worked as Assistant to the Director of Protocol for President Carter's Inauguration and I was most happy that President Carter was the first sitting President of the United States to visit Nigeria.

By going and spending time with African countries, President Clinton has not only given better awareness, but also provided a window of opportunity for economic development between America and Africa. I especially applaud President Clinton for going to Nigeria because there has been so much propaganda concerning Nigeria. I think his visits to Africa have broadened the base for diplomatic relations between many African countries and the United States as well as Nigeria. My prayer is that now President Clinton, who will soon leave office as the 42nd President of the United States, will continue to carry the banner of broadening the relationship between America and Africa, especially the country of Nigeria.

Sister Claudette
Marie Muhammad
Chief of Protocol
to the Honorable
Minister Louis Farrakhan
Deputy National Director of the Million Family March

Sister Claudette Marie Muhammad, Chief of Protocol to the Honorable Minister Louis Farrakhan, with her granddaughter, Tiffany Mayo, at the Million Family March on October 16, 2000.

"Thank God in my lifetime I have witnessed an American President who was sensitive to the needs of Africa and recognized the potential of a relationship with Africa."

Cathy Hughes
Chairman
Radio One, Inc.
(The first African American woman-owned
company on the New York Stock Exchange)

Photo Courtesy Kathy Hughes

Cathy Hughes, President of Radio One, Inc., and Susan Taylor, Publications Director for Essence Magazine. Radio One, Inc., is the first company owned by an African American woman to be listed on the New York Stock Exchange.

William Jefferson Clinton was "The People's President." His view, as Samuel "Sandy" Berger said in a recent edition of Foreign Affairs magazine, is truly global. Bill Clinton "recognized before many, that the most pervasive force in the world is globalization..." And that globalization, in full context, includes Africa. Bill Clinton saw that and acted on it.

President Clinton, and his dynamic life partner, now the Democratic Senator from New York, made it possible, for people of color to feel good about America, freeing Africans and African Americans from the margins.

The task that remains, particularly for those of us in media, is to charge and challenge ourselves with the task of building on the Clinton legacy, by continuing to open long closed doors of perception about Africa; to change the face of Africa in world media, and thus, the way the world thinks about Africa and Africans. Because of Bill Clinton its a new world, a world with Africa in it. And because of him, yesterday's roadmaps are all obsolete.

Tony Regusters
President
Capital City MediaWorks
and media consultant to the
African Communications Agency

Two great women, connecting greatness across the Atlantic. Pictured: American civil rights legend Rosa Parks, with Her Excellency Ruth Perry, former Interim President of Liberia.

Dr. Toni Luck, international representative for the Hebrew Israelites, poses with Dr. Erieka Bennett.

Without vision the people will perish, for according to the anointed, *Vision is Required In Order That One May Prepare or Develop According To One's Expectation for the Future.* As we look forward for the redemptive development of Africa, building upon the legacy of President Clinton, we must look to the sons and daughters of Africa to throw down the gauntlet and establish the works of righteousness in the land of creation, for it has been declared that the works of righteousness is peace. To that end we must look to men and women of vision, both individually and corporately, to assist in this epic struggle to build a righteous world, dedicated to the actual reality of lifted, peace and joy. At the critical state participation of those who can assist must be enlisted so that freedom and justice will be the heritage of all the children of creation Africa is truly the final frontier for, as the beginning of all life it is significant that now our attention should be turned back unto her for life and liberty.

Dr. Toni Luck
International Representation
Hebrew Israelites

Standing with Archbishop George A. Stallings, Jr., who is a friend of Africa, are students and Dr. Charles Beady, President, Piney Woods School, an African American boarding school in Jackson, Mississippi.

Vice President Al Gore, right, and the Coalition of Black Trade Unionists President William Lucy wave after addressing the Coalition of Black Trade Unionists.

Zainab Jaji, the Hon. Awwal Tukur (seated), and Isha Lami Danbauram. These are young, dynamic professional Africans, who travel internationally and are poised to continue the legacy from Africa.

President Clinton and C. Payne Lucas, President of Africare.

Abdul Latif Bennett, Chief Executive Officer of the African Communications Agency

President Clinton has brought about a welcome change in U.S.-Africa relations. We commend him for his efforts to promote peace and democracy and increase trade and economic development in Africa.

As countries around the world, including the United States, discover democracy has its challenges and opportunities, we will work with America to build strong governments and political systems throughout Africa. We thank him for his leadership and look forward to his continued dedication to improving U.S.-Africa relations. President Clinton's change in residence does not create a corresponding adjustment in my feeling that he is America's leader on U.S.-Africa relations.

Ted Turner, Time-Warner Vice President, left, talks with Percy Sutton, Chairman of African Continental Communications Telecommunnications Limited, and long-time NAACP member, during a telecommunications forum at the NAACP 89th Annual Convention in Atlanta.

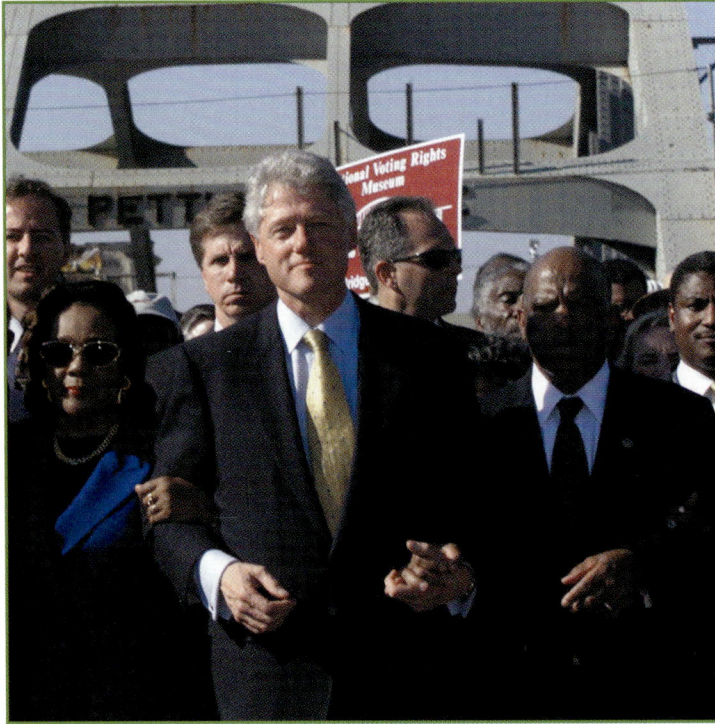

Photo Credit: J. Scott Applewhite/AP

President Clinton, center leads thousands of marchers across the Edmund Pettus Bridge in Selma, Alabama in celebration of the 35th anniversary of Bloody Sunday when Alabama state troopers beat marchers when they attempted to cross the bridge in a march to Montgomery seeking voting rights.

Photo Credit: Gene J. Puskar/AP

Coretta Scott King, second from right pays tribute to her friend, the late Betty Shabazz, at the NAACP's 88th Annual Convention. Joining King at the podium from left are Myrlie Evers-Williams, and two daughters of Betty Shabazz, Gamilah Shabazz and Ilyasah Shabazz.

Photo Credit: Wilfredo Lee/AP

President Clinton sings the national anthem with Kennedy Center Honorees Jacquis d' Amboise, Sidney Poitier and First Lady Hillary Rodham Clinton.

Photo Credit: Scott Applewhite/AP

President Clinton sits between the Rev. Jesse Jackson, left, and U.S. Rep. John Lewis, during ceremonies commemorating the 35th anniversary of Bloody Sunday.

For good reason, many consider House Judiciary Committee member Rep. Sheila Jackson Lee, (D-TX) one of Africa's most ardent supporters. Rep. Jackson-Lee traveled with President Clinton to Africa.

NAACP Chairwoman Myrlie Evers-Williams and President Clinton clasp hands at the 87th annual NAACP convention. Mrs. Evers-Williams, whose legacy as a champion of civil rights and social justice, was the widow of slain civil rights leader Medgar Evers.

107

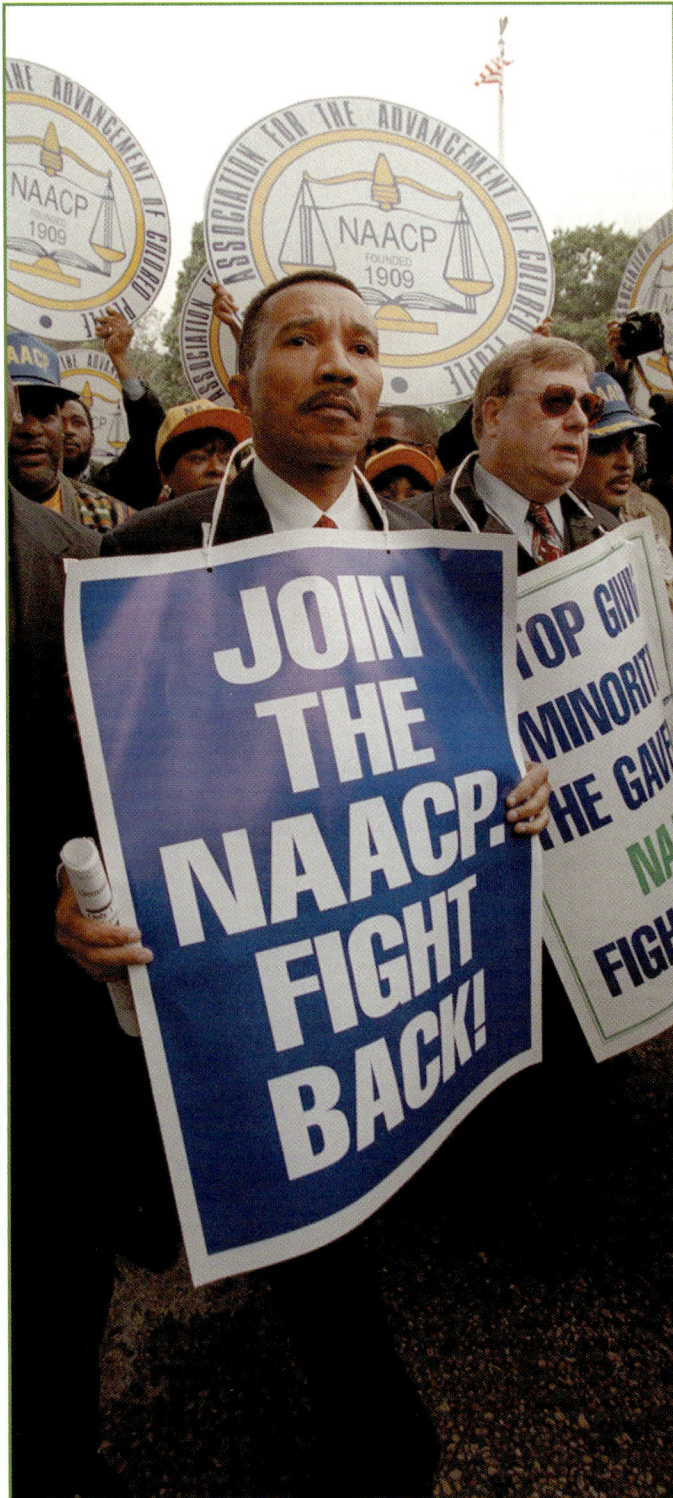

NAACP President Kweisi Mfume leads demonstrators at a march on the hiring of minority law clerks at the U.S. Supreme Court.

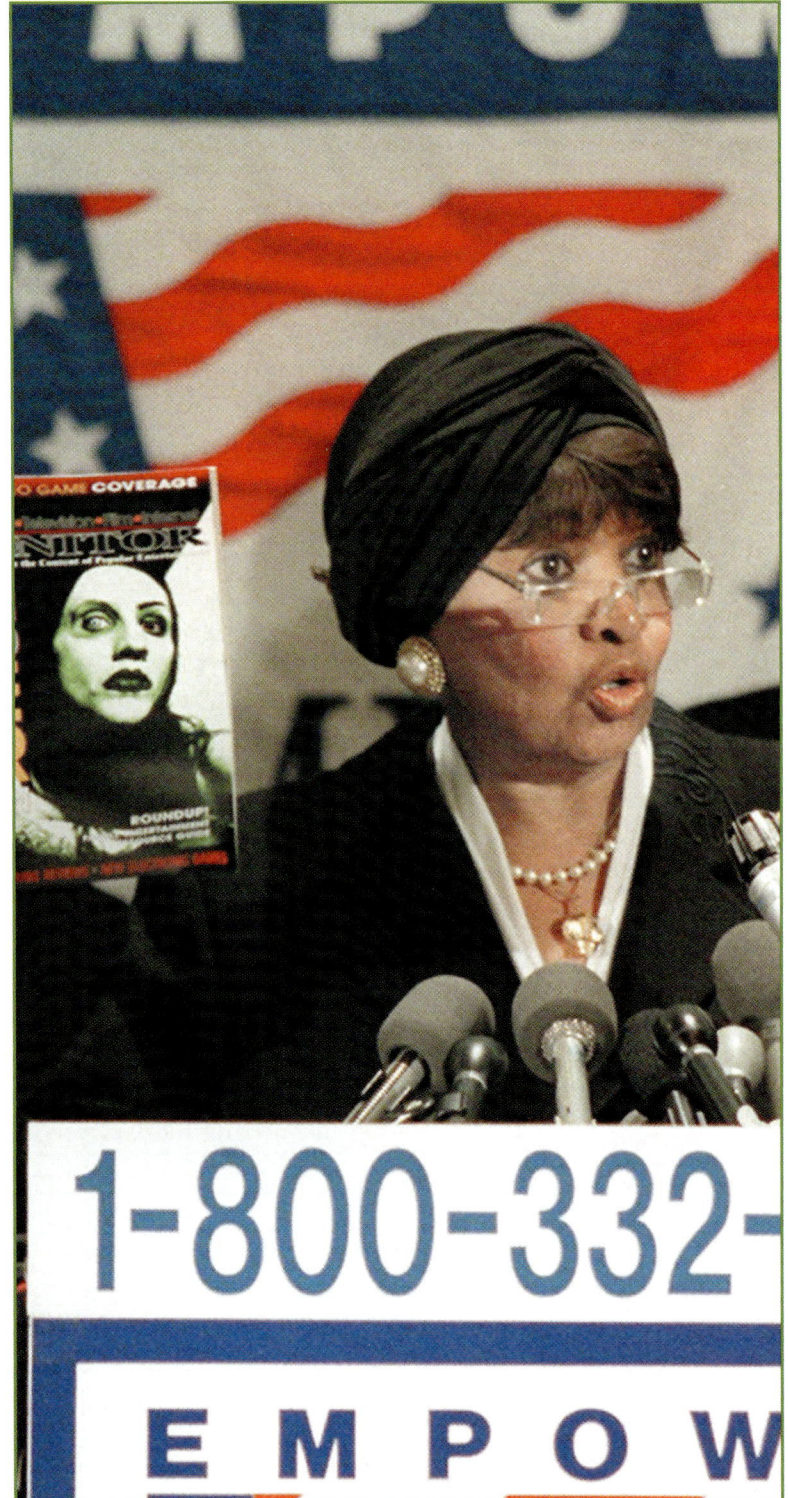

C. Dolores Tucker, Chairwoman, National Political Congress of Black Women, holds up a music magazine during a Washington news conference in May 1996.

Ben Ammi Ben Israel is the anointed Spiritual Leader of the African Hebrew Israelites of Jerusalem, which has a membership of about 3,000 in Israel and others in South Africa, Liberia, Ghana, and the Caribbean.

We made a lot of progress in terms of strengthening U.S. ties to Africa. Of course, President Clinton has played a major role in that. His Administration has decided that the world is important and Africa is a large part of that. We see a lot more interest from the U.S. to Africa. Africa is finally on the foreign policy map here in the United States.

I think democracy building is definitely a factor but I think there are other factors too. I think economic development – creating opportunity for people is a major spur. People need to have a stake in their own development. I think democracy is a by-product. If people are eating and people having jobs and people creating wealth in Africa, I think democracy will have a chance. If you don't have people eating, going to school and living normal lives, I don't think democracy will have any chance.

Mel Foote
President and CEO
Constituency for Africa

It was indeed an honor and a pleasure to work on this book, I did not realize that President Clinton had accomplished so much in eight years. This book was written to highlight the essence of Bill Clinton that superseded politics or geographic boundaries. He really has soul and this is very evident in the way he relates to people of color.

Dr. Erieka Bennett
Publisher, "The Legacy"
Vice-Chairperson, ACA

Photo Courtesy of ACA

Congressman William Jefferson (D-LA) (left), Archbishop George A. Stallings, Jr. (right), and Dr. Erieka Bennett at the Embassy of Nigeria.

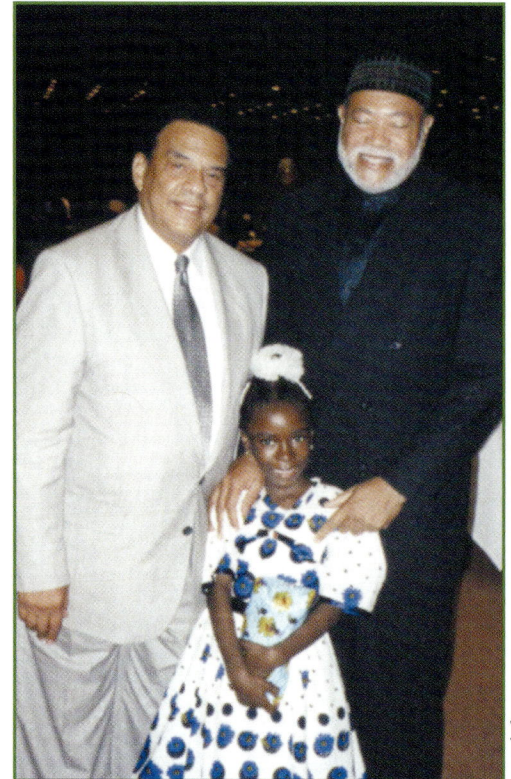

Photo Courtesy of ACA

Former Ambassador Andrew Young with Ed Davis and his daughter, Malca.

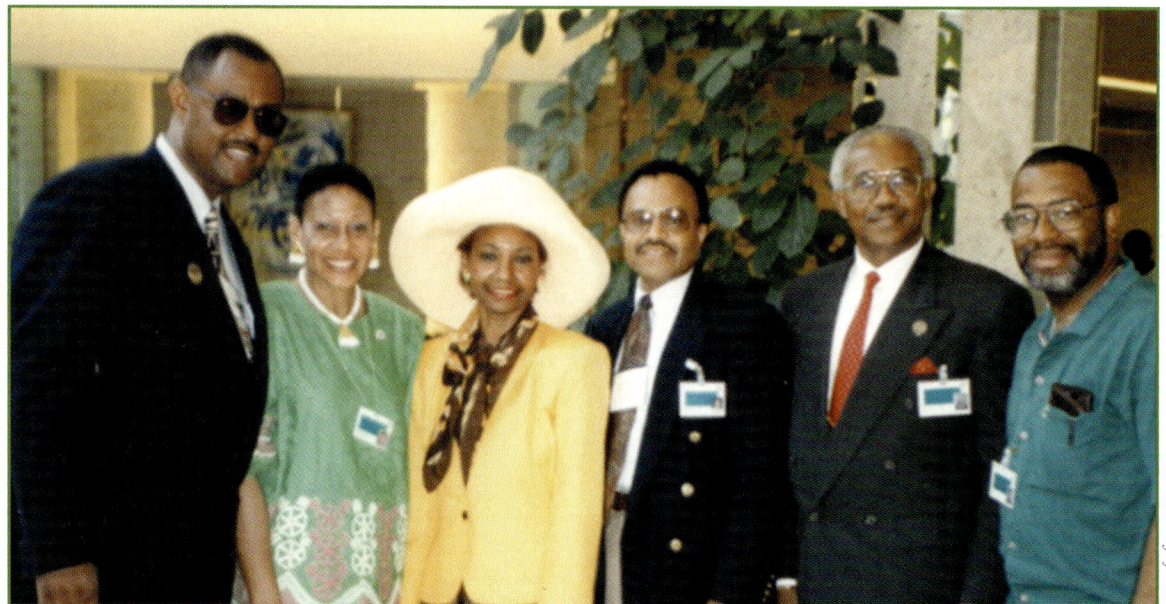

Photo Courtesy of ACA

Mel Foote (left), President of Constituency for Africa, and Alice Dear (second from left), former U.S. Executive Director of the African Development Bank, pose with other delegates at the African African American Summit.

Children's Defense Fund President Marian Wright Edelman addresses attendees of the Call to Renewal luncheon in Washington, DC in 1996. The Call to Renewal group was formed by nearly 100 religious leaders to counter the influence of the religious right.

Callisto Madavo, vice president of the World Bank for Africa, speaks to the media on the eve of the 13th International Conference on AIDS in Durban, South Africa.

President and Mrs. Clinton returning to The White House.

These are Companies and People
Who Can Help Sustain the Legacy

Photo Credits: George Widman/AP

The Prize in the Eyes. *President Clinton greets talk show host, motion picture star and magazine publisher Oprah Winfrey at the President's Call to Action Rally in Philadelphia, as former Presidents Gerald Ford, left, and George Bush, right, look on.*

Pharmaceuticals, Credit, Investment, and Telecommunications. *Charles A. Heinbold, Jr. (left), Chairman and CEO, Bristol-Myers, with Kenneth Chenault, President and COO, American Express (center), and Ivan Seidenberg, Chairman and CEO, Bell Atlantic (right).*

Oil: The Lifeblood of Global Industry and Commerce. *Africa provides eight percent of the oil imported to the United States. Lee Raymond is Chairman and CEO of Exxon Mobil Corporation.*

Hands Across the Skies. *African nations want and deserve safe and friendly skies. Pictured are Delta Airlines executives Lee F. Mullin, President and Chief Executive Officer, left, Gerald Grinstein, Executive Chairman of the Board, center, and Maurice Worth, Chief Operating Officer, right, clasp hands over a model of a Delta jet following a news conference at the company's Atlanta headquarters.*

Africa Needs Drugs and Medicines. *The battle continues against disease and HIV/AIDS, and international pharmaceutical companies have a big role to play. Pictured are Carl-Gustag Johansson, left, President and CEO of Astra Pharmaceuticals, with Judy Lewent, senior vice-president and CEO of Merck Co., and Hakan Mogren, Astra President and CEO.*

After Debt Relief, Africa Needs Investment and Development. *As sub-Saharan African nations restructure and realign their economies and balance trade on the model of the African Growth and Opportunity Act, American, European and Asian investment firms should open doors to new opportunities.   Pictured are Sir Richard Sykes, Chairman of Glaxo Wellcome, second left, and Jean-Pierre Garnier, Chief Executive Officer of SmithKline Beecham third left, with John Coombe, left, Finance Director of Glaxo Wellcome and Chief Financial Officer of the merged company, and Jan Leschly, right, former Chief Executive Officer of SmithKline.*

Africa Needs Bold Ideas and Action from African American Entrepreneurs. *Robert Johnson, Founder of Black Entertainment Television and creator of America's first black-owned airline (D.C. Air) has been a visionary entrepreneur and a long-time supporter and sustainer of African and African American issues.*

Africa, America, and the World of the 21st Century. *In the first decade of this new century, African and American business leaders can set a dynamic tone that can influence the next one hundred years. Pictured are American Express President Ken Chenault, left, and the company's Chairman and Chief Executive Officer, Harvey Golub, at American Express headquarters in New York.*

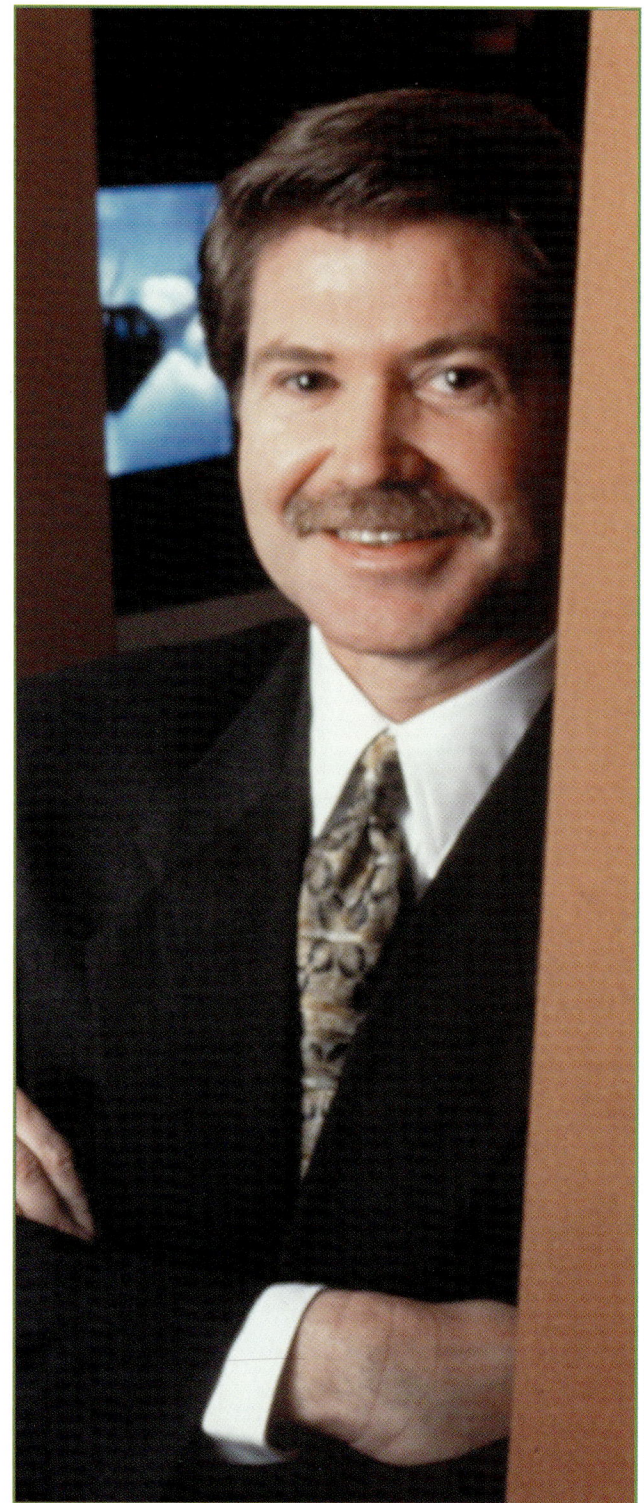

Bring Programming Excellence to Africa! *John Hendricks is founder and CEO, Discovery Communications.*

Giving Back, and Raising the Bar. *American companies like Chevron which recently merged with Texaco to become the world's fourth largest oil company, can set new standards for how business should be done in Africa. Chevron Corp's Chief Executive Officer, David J. O'Reilly, center, arrives for the investors' meeting with Texaco in New York.*

Champions of Peace and the New Prosperity. *Former President Jimmy Carter and Rosalynn Carter with Ted Turner, founder of CNN and Turner Broadcasting Network (right). Turner pledged part of his vast corporate fortune to benefit the United Nations Foundation.*

Wall Street! Make the 21st Century the Century of Africa! *With returns of more than 30 percent on investments, Wall Street has an opportunity to create a tremendous win-win windfall by encouraging investment in Africa. Pictured are Richard Grasso, Chairman and CEO of the New York Stock Exchange (left), Peter Kann, right, Chairman and Chief Executive Officer of Dow Jones and Co., and Jack Welch, Chairman and CEO of General Electric.*

American Oil Companies are Welcome in Africa. *Bringing American values and technology to African oil companies, Texaco (which recently merged with Chevron Corp) can help many African nations modernize and improve their civil and commercial infrastructures. Pictured is Peter Bijur, Chairman and Chief Executive Officer of Texaco.*

Future Vision: Electric Cars and Monorails in Africa. *General Motors has unveiled an energy-saving electric-vehicle, the EV-1. Africa could be an excellent market for this new car. Pictured is General Motors Chairman John Smith.*

Photo Credit: Ruth Fremson/AP

Two Champions, One in Politics, One in Sports. *President Clinton watches as basketball great Michael Jordan tees off at the Las Vegas Country Club, Las Vegas, Nevada.*

Photo Credit: Alan Diaz/AP

Sisters and Power Players. *Internationally renowned tennis stars Serena and Venus Williams are examples of Afrocentric prowess and power, on and off the court.*

"Tiger, Tiger, burning bright..." An avid golfer, President Clinton talks with record-making golf great Tiger Woods, and U.S. team captain Ken Venturi during opening ceremonies of the President's Cup Golf Tournament.

Photo Credit: Oscar Abolfha/AP

Imagine This! African children's television programming, sponsored by Toys "R" Us/Africa. *Africans are highly skilled craftsmen. These skills can easily be applied to toy-making and manufacturing. Pictured are Toys "R" Us President and Chief Executive Officer John Eyler and Discovery Communications, Inc., President and COO Judith McHale.*

Photo Credit: Kamenko Pajic/AP

Encourage Dialogue Between America's Best, Reaching Out to Africa. *Pictured are Michigan Governor John Engler, right, W. Franks Fountain, National Vice President for Governmental Affairs, DaimlerChrysler Corp., center, and Michigan District Court Judge Michael Martone.*

African Opportunities. *Gregory Hyson, Senior Vice President, Telesis Corporation, hopes to explore real estate development opportunities on the continent.*

> As a real estate developer, I am excited about the enormous potential for development opportunities in Africa. Residential and commercial real estate development are essential to building a viable economy in any country in the 21st century. African countries are not an exception. In fact, the opportunities in Africa are exceptional because of its vast, beautiful, and diverse land.
>
> As the second largest continent, Africa has enormous potential to become one of the hottest markets for real estate in the world. With a growth rate of three percent per year - higher than any other continent - all of its infrastructure sectors, especially housing and commercial real estate development, will take on even greater importance.
>
> I commend President Clinton for beginning the legacy. However, American and African business men and women have a responsibility as well to continue the legacy.
>
> *Gregory Hyson*
> *Senior Vice President*
> *Telesis Corporation*

Photo Credit: M. Butterfield / Telesis Corp.

A Champion for Global Peace. U.N. Secretary-General Kofi-Annan has been an eloquent and effective model for Africa's emerging cadre of young, 21st century leaders.

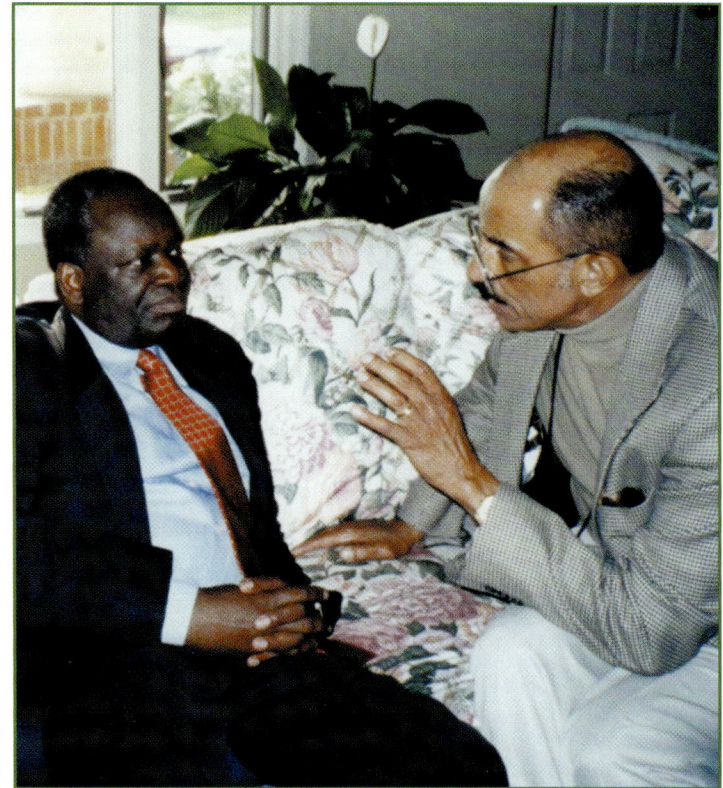

Professor Ibrahim Gambari, Under Secretary General and Special Advisor to the Secretary General on African Affairs at the United Nations, discussing African affairs with Retired General Fred Leigh, former head of Maritime Services in Liberia.

Nigerian AIDS Prevention Initiative. *The Bill & Melinda Gates Foundation awarded a $25 million grant through the Harvard School of Public Health (HSPH) in collaboration with the Harvard Center for International Development for execution of a program on HIV/AIDS prevention in Nigeria. Known as the Nigerian AIDS Prevention Initiative, the program will begin by profiling the nature of HIV infection in Nigeria. Researchers will then target prevention programs, as HSPH has done successfully for many years in Senegal, where infection rates have remained stable at two percent.*

In the past many Africans didn't always feel that Washington listens, Washington cares, or that Washington is concerned. Here's a President that said, I want African issues to come to me and I want to promote a partnership for the mutual benefit to both countries as partners and friends. The new Administration should build where President Clinton left off, which is to build on issues of trade, peacekeeping and in establishing true partnerships.

Professor Ibrahim Gambari
Under Secretary General and Special Advisor to
Secretary General on African Affairs
United Nations

Corporate References

New York Stock Exchange
11 Wall Street
New York, NY 10005-1905
212/656-3000

American Express
World Financial Center
New York, NY
212/964-7974

American Express
7 World Trade Center
New York, NY 10048-1102
212/964-7922

BET
1899 9th Street, NE
Washington, DC 20018-1050
202/259-9436

Chevron Companies
1325 Avenue of the Americas
New York, NY 10019-6026
212/424-2100

Delta Airlines
1001 International Blvd.
Atlanta, GA 30354-1802
404/761-6546

Enron Corp.
1400 Smith Street
Houston, TX 77002
713/853-6161

Exxon USA
23050 Pacific Blvd.
Sterling, VA 20166-9546
703/481-8637

World Bank
1818 H Street, NW
Washington, DC 20433-0001
202/477-1234

Merck & Company, Inc.
100 Corporate Drive
Lebanon, NJ 0833-2200
908/236-5000

Smithkline Beecham
467 W. Deming Place
Chicago, IL 60614-0986
773/477-0986

Oprah Winfrey
Chicago, IL
312/591-9595

Daimler Chrysler Corp.
110 Denbar Rd.
Bloomfield Hills, MI 48304-2731
248/593-6586

General Motors Corporation
1 General Motors Drive
Syracuse, NY 13206-1116
716/647-7000

Toys 'R' Us
38 Wolf Road
Albany, NY 12205-2603
518/459-5561

Mobil Oil Corp.
Halifax Lane
Chesapeake, VA 23320-0000
757/545-4681

These are companies and people who may or may not have interest or involvement in Africa.
Our intent is to focus on corporations who can help continue the legacy.

Former President of Tanzania, the late Julius Nyerere, speaks during a press conference in Arusha, Tanzania.

The *Spirit* of the Legacy

Some Africans and Americans did not get to see the culmination of President Clinton's mission to promote peace and democracy, foster trade and economic development, and strengthen human and infrastructure development in Africa. Many of these people, like Julius Nyerere, former president of Tanzania, and Ronald Brown, former U.S. Secretary of Commerce, helped to lay the groundwork for peace and democracy in Africa and improved trade between that continent and the United States.

Their spirits flow through this U.S.-Africa movement and live in all of the people who worked with them over the years. While they are not here physically, President Clinton and the heads of many African nations often speak of their wise counsel, intellect, and love for Africa.

There are numerous other individuals who labored tirelessly behind the scenes. These quiet laborers are often the spokes

in the wheel. While we do not list their names, their work lives in the dreams, hopes, and aspirations of Africa's people and all who continue to toil in the vineyards of the U.S.-Africa movement.

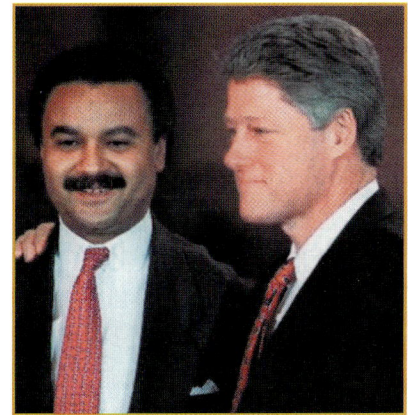

President Clinton and the late Ron Brown.

Photo Credit: Danny Johnstone/AP

Great leaders are often the products of supportive and loving parents, family members, and communities. Therefore, we also honor the spirit of President Clinton's mother, Virginia Kelley. While she is not here physically, the love and compassion she instilled in President Clinton are evident in everything that he does to serve all Americans and the people of the world.

President Clinton hugs his mother, the late Virginia Kelley, as his step-father Richard Kelley looks on during the Arkansas Ball.

The late Dr. Betty Shabazz, widow of Malcolm X, speaks on the steps of City Hall in New York as part of a rally calling for racial harmony.

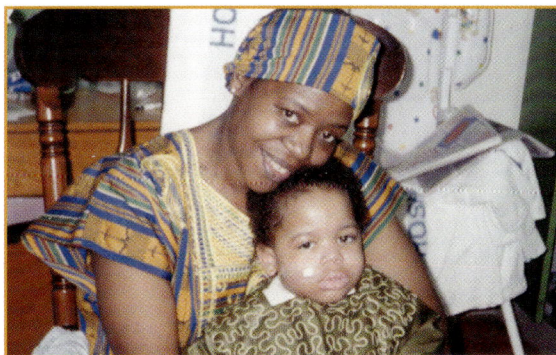

Jackie Jackson holds her son, Theo Jackson, who died of AIDS. We honor him and all the children and adults who have died of HIV/AIDS.

The late Ron Brown greets Esom Alintah of the African Business Roundtable.

The late Arthur Langford, a former Georgia State Senator, traveled throughout Africa reciting his version of the "I Have A Dream" speech by Dr. Martin L. King, Jr.

"The objectives of the African Business Roundtable are to speak for the private sector, promote its welfare, encourage inter-African trade and attract foreign investment for development purposes and perhaps, most importantly, it tries to change the awful perception abroad that Africa is a hopeless continent. Ron Brown was instrumental in helping us in this endeavor.

The Late Esom Alintah Founding member and former Secretary General African Business Roundtable"

President Clinton meets with members of his Cabinet.

The People Behind the Policies

Government Agencies Fostering Trade and Economic Development

Under President Clinton's leadership, Cabinet-level initiatives and programs to improve trade and economic development throughout Africa increased tremendously. In fact, most of the members of the Cabinet visited Africa at least once. And, as a result of President Clinton's leadership and the Cabinet-level visits, new trade and economic initiatives for Africa have been developed by the U.S. Departments of Commerce and Treasury as well as the Export-Import Bank, the Trade Development Agency, the Overseas Private Investment Corporation and the Office of the U.S. Trade Representative.

The **Department of Commerce** serves as the main catalyst for engaging the U.S. business community in Africa. The vision, energy, hope, and enthusiasm for Africa of the late Secretary of Commerce, Ron Brown, permeated the agency during his tenure and continued throughout the Administration. Not only did Ron Brown visit Africa numerous times, but so have the Secretaries of Commerce who followed him.

In December 1998, Commerce Secretary William Daley led a Presidential Business Development Mission to South Africa, Kenya, Nigeria, and Côte d'Ivoire. During the mission, the National Institute of Standards and Technology (a Department of Commerce administration) signed a Memorandum of Understanding with the Kenyan Government that provides a mechanism for scientific and technical cooperation in chemistry, physics, and engineering management services and standards related measures.

The mission included Commerce Department officials and 15 U.S. companies. The Department also co-sponsored a West African Legal Conference with the African Development Bank. During Secretary Daley's tenure, he visited Africa five times.

Other Department of Commerce initiatives include:

- Implementing the Manufacturing Technology Cooperation venture with South Africa's Center for Industrial and Scientific Research on behalf of majority business.

- Working with the U.S. Agency for International Development to establish commercial law development programs with selected African countries, providing training and consultative services to lawmakers, regulators, judges, lawyers, and educators on implementing market oriented commercial law systems.

- The International Trade Administration (ITA) Africa Office convened trade briefings for visiting African officials and decision makers emphasizing intellectual property rights and the negative impact of corruption on trade and development.

- Working with the Corporate Council on Africa, the ITA arranged the first U.S.-African Ambassadors' Tour of U.S. cities.

- The Foreign Commercial Service expanded its South African presence beyond Johannesburg with the addition of new offices in Cape Town and Durban. The President's FY 2000 Budget included $4.2 mil-

President Clinton and Vice President Al Gore pose with African Americans who were on the White House staff in 1998.

Photo Credit: White House

lion to hire 12 new Foreign Commercial Service Officers in Africa.

- ITA's Advocacy Center is helping American firms win African contracts by organizing high-level U.S. government advocacy on behalf of U.S. companies. Since its creation in 1995, the Advocacy Center has assisted U.S. firms in winning 38 contract awards in Africa, worth a total of approximately $2.7 billion.

The **Department of Transportation** launched the Transportation Initiative and Partnership with Africa under the theme, "Transportation: The Tie That Binds." The partnership focuses on the vital importance of developing safe and efficient transportation systems to Africa's continued economic development.

During President Clinton's historic 1998 Africa tour, U.S. Secretary of Transportation Rodney Slater was the only Cabinet member to accompany the President on the entire

Photo Credit: Susan Walsh/AP

President Clinton, flanked by Secretary of Transportation Rodney Slater, left, and Detroit NAACP President Reverend Wendell Anthony, waves to the crowd before delivering his remarks to the 45th Annual Fight for Freedom Fund Dinner in Detroit.

trip, where he pursued a successful agenda to benefit U.S.-Africa transportation issues. In Ghana, he signed a $67 million loan guarantee for the purchase of two barge-mounted power plants to be constructed in the United States and delivered to Ghana. In Botswana, the Secretary joined USAID Administrator Brian Atwood in signing a contract with an American company to install a computerized rail car tracking system that will link up eight key railroads in Southern Africa.

In July 1997, Secretary Slater and the Reverend Jesse Jackson co-led the U.S. delegation to the Fourth African-African American Summit in Harare, Zimbabwe. And Secretary Slater has been instrumental in advancing the President's partnership in the United States. In October 1997, Secretary Slater hosted the U.S.-Africa Roundtable on Trade and Investment, which brought together nearly 300 representatives from the U.S. government, the private sector, non-governmental organizations, and the African Diplomatic Corps to discuss U.S.-Africa relations. In December 1997, Secretary Slater met with Miami-area business executives to discuss private sector opportunities in Africa and how the administration's initiatives support U.S. businesses doing business on the continent.

A major goal of the Transportation Department's Africa initiative is also to assist Africa's emergence into the global marketplace in aviation. To help achieve this goal, a civil aviation team, with members of the Office of the Secretary of Transportation and the Federal Aviation Administration, traveled to Africa to engage in a series of meetings with African aviation officials. During this trip, discussions focused on the need for enhanced aviation safety and security in Africa, prospects for future aviation liberalization, and the possibilities for code share agreements.

Other initiatives under the Department of Transportation include:

- The Federal Highway Administration (FHWA) has worked in partnership with the South African Department of Transportation to establish a technology transfer (T2) center in Pretoria. This center helps local officials select technologies that meet their specific needs in building and maintaining their roads. With the support of the FHWA another technology transfer center has been established in Dar es Salaam, Tanzania.

> The United States and Nigeria today concluded an "Open Skies Agreement" that will expand and enhance the overall aviation partnership between the two countries. A total of 47 such agreements have been signed by the U.S., all but one under my administration.
>
> *President*
> *William Jefferson Clinton*
> *Remarks to Nigerian*
> *Business Leaders*
> *August 28, 2000*

President Clinton, flanked by Vice President Gore, Cabinet officials, and members of his economic team, meets with reporters in the Rose Garden.

- The Federal Railroad Administration (FRA) has also become involved in technology-sharing programs in Africa. The FRA also worked with the World Bank, the National Imagery and Mapping Agency and other Transportation Administrations to develop a CD-ROM for the African continent to simulate rail, traffic forecasts, and economic modeling.

- The National Highway Traffic Safety Administration (NHTSA) is working with the World Bank and others on a proposed road safety program.

- The Federal Transit Administration (FTA) is working to develop transportation education curricula that will be made available to African transit interests and educational institutions. The FTA also initiated development of training materials and safety-related training in South Africa.

- The Federal Aviation Administration provides classroom and on-the-job training to aviation officials from numerous African countries through its international Training Services Center at the FAA Academy in Oklahoma City.

- The U.S. Coast Guard provides assistance to several African countries through U.S. resident training and Mobile Training Teams that focus on areas such as maritime law enforcement, search and rescue, marine environmental protection, and port safety and security.

In addition to its focus on peace, human rights, and democracy, the **State Department** posted an additional Foreign Service Officer in Nigeria to work with federal and state governments, Niger Delta communities, and private companies. This additional posting will help improve and coordinate efforts by the Nigerian government to ensure that the region's people benefit more equitably from Nigeria's economic resources growth and development.

In support of the President's partnership, the **Department of Treasury** leads U.S. participation in the International Financial Institutions (IFIs) -- the International Monetary Fund, the World Bank, and the African Development Bank. IFIs provide the major sources of financing and technical assistance aimed at

President Clinton and First Lady Hillary Rodham Clinton pose with Alice Dear, former U.S.Executive Director of the African Development Bank.

"I thank President Clinton for the opportunity he gave me to play a really important role in shaping what was happening in Africa through my role as the U.S. Executive Director of the African Development Bank. I've been involved in Africa for 30 years, traveling to Africa for 30 years, and have always felt very close to the Continent. I was ahead of my time and for a great deal of that period people thought I was very, very weird. The President gave me a voice to continue to advocate for Africa.

I also thank him for following his heart and really sharing sincere feelings that he has for the continent. A sincere belief that the continent does matter, it matters to Americans, it matters to the world, and for doing what he could to push the envelope on this, to use his position as President of the only super power in the world to show that this continent is important and that we want it as a trade partner and that had never been said before. Even before the trade aspects, the security issues were important and our legacy probably wasn't so good in terms of involvement in Somalia, and it hampered the U.S. from getting involved in Rwanda. I think he made a good gesture in admitting that we probably should have acted sooner. I don't think you often hear leaders express any kind of contriteness for decisions that were made.

Alice Dear
Former U.S. Executive Director
African Development Bank"

strengthening sub-Saharan African economic institutions, supporting human development, and encouraging more open investment and trade regimes. The IFIs created a joint Africa Institute in Cote d'Ivoire to train African officials in economic management and policy development.

The U.S. Department of Treasury will also provide technical assistance to the Nigerian government in budget and fiscal policy and government debt issuance and management. In July 1998, Secretary Robert Rubin became the first Secretary of the Treasury in U.S. history to tour Africa, visiting South Africa, Cote d'Ivoire, Kenya, Namibia, and Mozambique.

The **Office of the U.S. Trade Representative** (USTR) is responsible for developing closer trade and investment relations with Africa by negotiating agreements, offering trade incentives for reform, and finding common interests. The USTR has negotiated three landmark Trade and Investment Framework Agreements (TIFAs) with South Africa and

Rev. Jesse Jackson gives a thumbs up on arriving with National Security Adviser Sandy Berger, right, at the Presidential Palace in Dakar, Senegal.

J. Scott Applewhite/AP

Ghana, and a Bilateral Investment Treaty (BIT) with Mozambique. The South Africa TIFA was the first with a sub-Saharan African country. TIFAs provide a framework for discussing specific trade and investment matters, negotiating new agreements, and working to remove trade and investment barriers. BITs are market-opening agreements that protect U.S. investment abroad, and help to attract investment by ensuring predictable environments for investment guided by market forces.

The USTR has also worked with the Agency for International Development and the Department of Agriculture to design a series of national and regional workshops to develop World Trade Organization (WTO) expertise in Africa and to help African countries understand the WTO and potential benefits resulting from additional commitments. In December 1998, the first WTO workshops were held in Zambia and South Africa.

The **U.S. Trade and Development Agency** (TDA) is an independent agency that funds feasibility studies, consultancies, training programs and other business project planning services in emerging market countries. After years of inactivity in Nigeria, TDA signed its first grant agreement on July 26, 2000 for an important sugar industry feasibility study project in northern Nigeria. TDA also approved funding for projects totaling more than $1.6 million for expansion of Nigerian use of domestic natural gas, refinery

modernization to produce upgraded fuels for the Nigerian market, development of a major new cement factory, and management of the radio frequency spectrum for telecommunications access. These commitments could lead to the development of nearly $1 billion in investments in crucial economic sectors.

The **Export Import Bank** (EX-IM) provides direct loans, guarantees and credit insurance to private and public sector African companies that wish to import American products. EX-IM also provides working capital to American companies that export. EX-IM extended routine financing for U.S. exports to 11 sub-Saharan African countries through a new Africa Pilot Program that makes short-term insurance available in countries where routine EX-IM financing is currently unavailable. The countries impacted by the new Africa Pilot Program are: Chad, Equatorial Guinea, Guinea, Madagascar, Malawi, Mauritania, Mozambique, Nigeria, Tanzania and Togo.

Overseas Private Investment Corporation (OPIC) programs are available in 38 of the 48 countries in Sub Saharan Africa. In 1997, OPIC launched a $150 million Modern Africa Growth and Investment Fund in response to proposals initiated by Congress and the Administration focusing on manufacturing, mining, and telecommunications. Another $120 million New Africa Opportunity Fund is now fully capitalized and investing in Southern Africa. The direct impact of

Dr. Enyantu Ifenne, Nigeria Director for Population Activities, left, President Clinton, Rep. Carolyn Maloney, D-NY, and Secretary of State Madeleine Albright, right, walk to the East Room at the White House.

Photo Credit: Joe Marquette/AP

OPIC Funds in Africa has been $1 billion in U.S. exports over five years, 1,800 U.S. jobs, $900 million in additional investments, $126 million in annual revenues to African countries, and 7,500 African jobs.

Created in 1971 as an independent agency of the U.S. government, OPIC seeks to mobilize and facilitate participation of U.S. private capital and skills in developing countries and emerging markets.

Daniel Glickman, Secretary of the **Department of Agriculture (USDA)**, also established a bilateral agreement with Ghana during the February 1999 State visit of President Rawlings. The agreement focuses on rural development, agricultural research, conservation and trade and business development. A two-year program has also been established to explore the markets for export of U.S. hardwoods to South Africa and to provide the South African carpentry industry with seminars on the properties and uses of U.S. hardwoods and component parts.

In February 1999, USDA presented a "Regionalization" policy to the South African government that allows imports of South African cattle from regions of the country free of animal or plant diseases, which had been prohibited.

Through the U.S. Agency for International Development, the **Africa Trade and Investment Policy (ATRIP) Program** is providing assistance to help reform-oriented African countries improve the environment for trade and private investment to catalyze relationships between U.S. and African firms, through business linkages, business associations and networks; and to help finance implementation of aggressive, market-friendly reforms.

Photo Credit: Greg Gibson/AP

President Clinton shakes hands with former Agriculture Secretary Mike Espy.

First Lady Hillary Clinton points to a rainbow that has formed over the water at Victoria Falls, Zimbabwe. President and Mrs. Clinton often focused on human and infrastructure development issues, including the environment.

Government Agencies Strengthening Human and Infrastructure Development

Several government agencies and departments have implemented community- and infrastructure-based programs in support of President Clinton's Partnership for Economic Growth and Opportunity in Africa. The following programs are examples:

The **U.S.-Africa Energy Partnership Initiative** introduced by Secretary Richardson on April 1, 1999, focuses on the need for African countries and regional organizations to integrate energy infrastructure; to develop partnership among governments, industry, non-government organizations and universities; to foster economic development; and to increase U.S.-Africa energy cooperation. A cornerstone of the Energy Partnership Initiative was the U.S.-Africa Energy Ministers Conference in December 1999. This conference represented the first time energy officials from Africa and the United States convened as a collective body to discuss the future of Africa's energy sector. Representatives from 48 countries participated in the conference.

The U.S.-Africa Energy Ministers Conference produced six new energy initiatives with African countries.

U.S.-Africa Sustainable Energy Program. DOE signed a Memorandum of Understanding (MOU) with the Overseas Private Investment Corporation (OPIC) to create the U.S. - Africa Sustainable Energy Program to assist U.S. not-for-profit entities, non-governmental organizations (NGOs), and small business entities or cooperatives in developing sustainable energy projects in Africa. DOE and OPIC will help identify financing opportunities for projects that meet program criteria.

Conference on Sustainable Energy Technologies for Africa. DOE will co-host, with an African partner, a Conference on Sustainable Energy Technologies. The conference will help increase the region's understanding of key climate change programs and identify opportunities and projects for U.S. and African business interests, such as geothermal and wind energy systems.

Following a speech at Shaw University, former Energy Secretary Hazel O'Leary displays a photo of President and Mrs. Clinton and the President of Shaw University, Dr. and Mrs. Talbert Shaw. She was instrumental in starting some U.S. energy initiatives in Africa.

Oil Spill Response Workshop. DOE, together with the International Maritime Organization (IMO) and interested African countries, will plan an oil spill response workshop to help develop national and regional capabilities to plan and respond to oil spill emergencies and help support growing environmentally sustainable investment in petroleum exploration and production. The workshop seeks to assess existing capacity, determine needs, and establish a framework to promote a cost-effective response system for Africa. Concurrent with the workshop, DOE will work with the Department of Commerce to co-sponsor an event focused on environmentally sound oil exploration, development and transportation technologies.

Capacity Building Initiative. DOE and the University of Houston's Energy Institute are developing a two week

Energy Secretary Bill Richardson announced the U.S.-Africa Energy Initiative on April 1, 1999.

training program "New Era for Oil and Gas Value Creation" to help African government energy officials address issues related to development of oil and gas sector supply, infrastructure and markets. Support for the program will come from industry partners and collaboration with the World Bank and other international organizations.

Summer Energy Institute at the University of Arizona. DOE and the University of Arizona are working to establish a Summer Energy Institute for African government energy officials. The Institute will follow-up on the themes of the U.S.-Africa Energy Ministers Conference and help participants develop the tools to create sustainable energy programs in Africa.

Technical Assistance for Southern Africa Development Community (SADC) Energy Commission. DOE and the U.S. Agency for International Development (USAID) will contribute $1.5 million. The projects will help promote competitive energy markets and a positive investment climate.

The **U.S. Environmental Protection Agency (EPA)** is currently involved in a variety of cooperative programs in South Africa. The agency provided solid waste management training and technical assistance to townships outside East London, South Africa and completed a solid waste characterization and market analysis for Duncan Village and the Greater East London area in South Africa.

In August 1998, 23 South Africans participated in a mining study tour. Participants had the opportunity to interact with their counterparts in the United States to discuss a variety of issues and topics surrounding mining and the management of mining wastes.

In May 2000, EPA hosted six representatives of South Africa's Environmental Justice Network Forum (EJNF) to exchange information and build networks with the American environmental justice community. The delegates visited U.S. communities facing environmental justice issues and participated in workshops and roundtable's with environmental justice leaders and community-based organizations. The program also provided an opportunity for the participants to meet with African American civil rights leaders and U.S. philanthropic foundations.

Under its Green Communities for Africa Strategy, the U.S. Environmental Protection Agency plans to expand its work to other African countries based on the success of current EPA activities in South Africa.

President Clinton's visit to the Victoria Mxenge Housing site in Guguletu, South Africa, had a significant impact on the **U.S. Agency for International Development's** (USAID) housing program in South Africa. A new grant was signed recently with People's Dialogue, a non-governmental organization that is assisting the community in Victoria Mxenge to build their homes. The three-year $500,000 grant will create

President and Mrs. Clinton react after her speech following a visit to Victoria Mxenge housing project in Guguletu, South Africa.

a housing revolving fund for the residents to build and improve their homes.

USAID has also established a primary health services decentralization pilot program that provided a model for moving beyond relief to development services in Rwanda. With the European Union, USAID implemented a major seeds/tools program that increased food production levels to approximately 60 percent of pre-war levels in Liberia and supported the Leland Initiative's School-to-School Partnership program. The Leland program is aimed at facilitating cross-cultural dialogue and joint projects between U.S. and African primary and secondary schools via the Internet.

President Clinton and First Lady Hillary Rodham Clinton greet schoolchildren during a visit to the East Rand Township of Thokoza, outside Johannesburg.

Former South African President Nelson Mandela, right, Vivian-Lowery Derryck of the U.S. Agency for International Development (USAID) in Africa, center, and U.S. Ambassador to South Africa, Delano Lewis, left, arrive at the 13th International AIDS Conference in Durban, South Africa.

The **U.S. Department of Labor (DOL)** is providing advice and technical assistance to labor ministries in sub-Saharan Africa and has initiated work in the region to promote core labor standards and eliminate the worst forms of child labor. To meet the challenges associated with transitioning economies, USDOL will work in partnership with African nations to enhance their commitment to core labor standards to sustain economic growth. USDOL provides technical assistance worldwide on labor market reform and development, with funding from USAID, the World Bank, and other multilateral development banks.

In 1998, the DOL provided grants to South Africa to conduct a nationwide child labor survey and to Uganda to assist the government in preparing for participation in the International Program to Eliminate the Worst Forms of Child Labor.

The **Federal Transit Administration (FTA)** developed training materials and provided safety-related training in South Africa. The initial results of the safety training program were encouraging and will be replicated in other African countries. Through resources and assistance

President Clinton and Ben Johnson, Assistant to the President and Director of the Initiative for one America, in a meeting with a broad group of American religious leaders at The White House to discuss their efforts to mobilize the faith community around the goal of building a discrimination-free America. Johnson also works with government agencies, the private sector, community organizations, and the general public in an effort to improve race relations in America.

provided by the National Transit Institute, University Transportation Centers and the Transportation Cooperative Research Program, FTA is working to develop transportation education curricula that will be made available to African transit interests and educational institutions.

The **U.S. Department of Agriculture (USDA)** has established an initiative for sub-Saharan African countries on Policy Approaches to Sanitary and Phytosanitary International Standards and Implementation. Under this initiative, approximately 20 sub-Saharan countries will participate in workshops to review food safety and WTO issues. Two similar workshops were completed in South Africa in 1998.

The Agriculture Research Service has undertaken a three-year project that will enable it and the International Institute for Tropical Agriculture in Benin to develop techniques to use strains of fungus to prevent contamination of corn by aflatoxin.

The Cochran Fellowship Program is providing short-term agricultural training programs in the United States for mid- and senior-level professionals in agricultural trade, marketing, management, policy and technology transfer. Fellows have come from Senegal, Côte d'Ivoire, South Africa, Kenya, Namibia, Ghana, Nigeria, and Uganda.

The USDA sponsored pavilions at the Food and Hotel Africa Trade Show in South Africa in 1996, 1998 and 2000. These pavilions provide an excellent opportunity for U.S. exporters to introduce their high-value food products to South African and neighboring markets. The USDA has also appointed a senior agricultural economist to function as project manager for the Famine Early Warning System in sub-Saharan Africa.

The **National Institutes of Health** received a $1 million grant to provide further assistance to the Multilateral Initiative on Malaria (MIM). The funded project will focus on continuing educational seminars and will support the Regional Malaria Lab in Mali to reinforce its position as a regional center of excellence in Africa. This effort will complement an ongoing Infectious Disease Initiative for Africa, emphasizing surveillance, response, prevention, and building local resistance capacity for infectious diseases throughout the continent.

These are main programs and policies initiated by President Clinton. There may be others that were not printed due to space limitations.

Singing the civil rights anthem, "We Shall Overcome," President Clinton holds hands with Ernest Green, center, and Jefferson Thomas, far left, at the conclusion of a Congressional Gold Medal ceremony in the White House.

Afterword

by Ernest G. Green

I had the privilege of accompanying President Clinton on part of his historic trip to Africa. I know that he was personally transformed by the visit. Moreover, I am convinced that it will be seen as a defining event in the history of relations between Africa and the United States. President Clinton defined a new framework and new philosophy, and he promised new relationships and new resources to assist Africa's political, social and economic development. This single but significant action transformed America's vision of Africa and defined a new tone and direction for our policy toward the continent.

In words and deeds, Bill Clinton has shown that Africa matters! History will view his tenure as a critical turning point in United States relations with this vast, beautiful continent. During his presidency, President Clinton has:

created a new atmosphere for U.S. relations with Africa, characterized by respect and mutually beneficial partnerships;

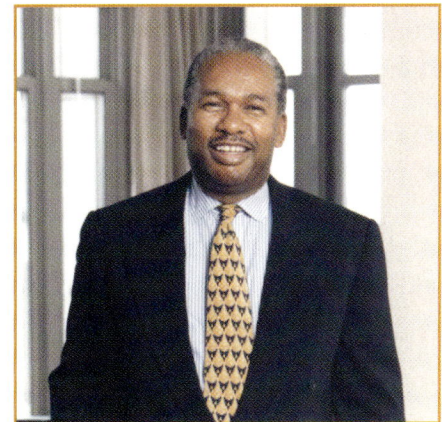

Ernest G. Green

established Africa's importance in U.S. foreign policy, based on clear, strong national strategic and economic interests; increased American assistance to tackle the continent's complex problems; leveraged billions of dollars in private investment and unlocked doors for global trade to stimulate Africa's economic development; galvanized public and private resources to tackle the AIDS problem in Africa; changed public perceptions and raised American consciousness about Africa and its people; and engendered a sense of pride among more than thirty million Americans, like myself, whose roots are in Africa.

President Clinton has a passion for Africa and for bringing peace and prosperity to the continent. His untiring commitment to forging a brighter future and closer partnerships with Africa are exemplified in four specific areas that I can address from first-hand experience with the President. He understands that people around the world yearn for justice and for equal opportunities to improve their lives.

During the early years of his administration, the President boldly marshaled international pressure against apartheid in South Africa and, with great foresight, mobilized American resources to train a cadre of black South Africans who could become future leaders in both the public and private sectors. The United States then invested tens of millions of dollars to ensure that South Africa's first open elections, in 1995, were free and fair. When Nelson Mandela was elected president, Mr. Clinton saluted him in a Rose Garden ceremony and committed $600 million in American assistance to extend education and health care to all South Africans and to stimulate broad economic growth.

Mr. Clinton wisely recognized that Nigeria and South Africa are Africa's pillars and are key to the continent's peace and prosperity. He played a strong, personal role in Nigeria, to help set a new path to democracy and prosperity following fifteen years of corrupt, military rule. President Clinton

committed the United States to partner with the new government of Olusegun Obasanjo to build democratic institutions and values and to stimulate economic growth, providing more than $100 million annually toward this end, which made Nigeria the largest American aid program in the world, after Egypt. When progress was slower than people's aspirations, President Clinton traveled to Nigeria in 2000 and powerfully encouraged the citizens to be patient, exhorting the arms of government to work together toward a common good.

President Clinton recognized early on the important contributions the American private sector could make toward Africa's development. With the fall of apartheid, he encouraged reinvestment in South Africa, promoting throughout his travels on the continent additional opportunities for U.S. investment. Bill Clinton took passage of the African Growth and Opportunity Act as a personal challenge. His goal was to generate jobs for Americans here at home while opening critical American markets to Africans.

President Clinton has a passion for promoting peace and prosperity for all people. Toward that end, he nominated me to serve as Chairman of the Board of the African Development Foundation. ADF has been an innovator in promoting African solutions and providing Africans with resources to solve their own problems. The Foundation supports many of the very things the President underscored during his tenure – alleviating poverty and promoting empowerment through small loans; therefore linking grassroots communities to global trade and investment to promote robust economic growth and protect Africa's fragile environment.

Each year, the Foundation's programs help grow thousands of small African-owned businesses, create tens of thousands of jobs, build hundreds of local institutions, and produce high-impact models for development that can be replicated by African communities and governments, and international development agencies. President Clinton continually proposed a growing budget for ADF to advance grassroots economic growth and empower poor communities and women, and also pressed for reinstating a separate Development Fund for Africa.

In Africa, as home, President Clinton has shown courageous, enlightened leadership. He has worked hard to open up political and economic systems, for the empowerment and benefit of *all* people. He recognized the unique opportunity offered by a new generation of African leaders to forge new partnerships and to promote innovative solutions to vexing age-old problems. The President set new directions for U.S. foreign policy and promoted new ways of mobilizing resources for Africa's development. Bill Clinton has established a strong foundation for future leaders – public and private – to build on, and benefit both Africa and the United States.

Ernest G. Green is Managing Director of Public Finance for Lehman Brothers, Washington, D.C. He was also appointed by President Clinton to serve as chairman of the African Development Foundation. Mr. Green, along with other former Little Rock High School students, was presented with the Congressional Gold Medal for his outstanding bravery during the integration of the school in 1957. Mr. Green is also a long-time friend of President Clinton.

Selected *Speeches* *by* President Clinton

Remarks by President Clinton at the Burundi Peace Talks
Simba Hall
Arusha International Conference Center
Arusha, Tanzania

August 28, 2000

Thank you very much, President Museveni, President Mkapa, distinguished leaders of the OAU and various African nations and other nations supporting this peace process. It is a great honor for me to be here today with a large delegation from the United States, including a significant number of members of our Congress, and my Special Envoy to Africa, Reverend Jesse Jackson and Howard Wolpe and others who have worked on this for a long time.

This is a special day in America and for Reverend Jackson. I think I should just mention it in passing. This is the 37th anniversary of the most important civil rights meeting we ever had: the great March on Washington, where Jesse Jackson was present and Martin Luther King gave his "I Have A Dream" speech. I say that not because I think the situations are analogous, but because everybody needs a dream, and I think whether you all decide to sign this or not depends in part on what your dream is.

I thank my friend, President Mandela, for coming in to replace the marvelous late President Nyerere, to involve himself in this process. After 27 years in prison and four years as President of his country — which some people think is another form of prison — he could be forgiven if he had pursued other things. But he came here because he believes in peace and reconciliation. He knows there is no guarantee of success; but if you don't try, there is a guarantee of failure. And failure is not an acceptable option.

So I thank him, I thank the OAU and, Mr. President, you are here today. I thank the regional leaders, in addition to Presidents Museveni and Mkapa, President Moi, President Kagame, Prime Minister Meles, for their work. I thank the Nyerere Foundation, Judge Bomani, Judge Warioba and I thank the people of Tanzania for hosting us here in a city that has become the Geneva of Africa, thanks to many of you.

I say again, I am honored to be in a place that is a tribute to the memory of President Nyerere, and I'm glad that Madam Nyerere is here today. I met her a few moments ago, and I thank her for her presence.

I thank President Buyoya and all the Burundians from all the parties who have come to Arusha and for the efforts you have made.

Peacemaking requires courage and vision — courage because there are risks involved, and vision because you have to see beyond the risks to understand that however large they are, they are smaller than the price of unending violence. That you have come so far suggests you have the courage and vision to finish the job, and we pray that you will.

I confess that I come here with some humility. I have spent a great deal of time in the last eight years trying to talk people into laying down their arms and opening their hands to one another — from the Middle East to Northern Ireland to the Balkans. I have had some measure of success and known some enormously painful failures. But I have not been here with you all this long time — and maybe I have nothing to add to your deliberations, but I would like to share some things that I have learned in eight years of seeing people die, seeing people fight with one another because they're of different ethnic or racial or tribal or religious groups, and of seeing the miracles that come from normal peace.

First, to state the obvious; there will be no agreement unless there is a compromise. People hate compromise because it requires all those who participate in it to be less than satisfied. So it is, by definition, not completely satisfying. And those who don't go along can always point their finger at you and claim that you sold out: Oh, it goes too fast in establishing democracy. Oh, it goes too slow in establishing democracy. It has absolutely too many protections for minority rights. No, it doesn't have enough protections for minority rights.

And there's always a crowd that never wants a compromise — a small group that actually would, by their own definition, at least, benefit from continued turmoil and fighting. So if you put the compromise on the table, they will use it like salt being rubbed into old wounds. And they're always very good. They know just where the break points are to strike fear into the hearts of people who have to make the hard decisions. I have seen this all over the world.

But I know that honorable compromise is important, and requires people only to acknowledge that no one has the whole truth, that they have made a decision to live together, and that the basic aspirations of all sides can be fulfilled by simply saying no one will be asked to accept complete defeat.

Now, no one ever compromises until they decide it's better than the alternative. So I ask you to think about the alternative. You're not being asked today to sign a comprehensive agreement, you're being asked to sign on to a process which permits you to specify the areas in which you still have disagreements, but which will be a process that we all hope is completely irreversible.

Now, if you don't do it, what is the price? If you don't do it, what is the chance that the progress you have made will unravel? If you come back in five or 10 years, will the issues have changed? I think not. The gulf between you won't narrow, but the gulf between Burundi and the rest of the world, I assure you, will grow wider if you let this moment slip away. More lives will be lost. And I have a few basic questions. I admit, I am an outsider. I admit,

I have not been here with you. But I have studied this situation fairly closely. I don't understand how continued violence will build schools for your children, bring water to your villages, make your crops grow, or bring you into the new economy. I think it is impossible that that will happen. Now, I do think it is absolutely certain that if you let this moment slip away, it will dig the well of bitterness deeper and pile the mountain of grievances higher, so that some day, when somebody else has to come here and sit at a table like this, they will have an even harder job than you do. So I urge you to work with President Mandela; I urge you to work with each other to seize the opportunity that exists right now.

And I urge those groups, including the rebels who are not now part of this process, to join it and begin taking your own risks for peace. No one can have a free ride here. Now that there is a process for resolving differences peacefully, they should lay down their arms.

Now, if you take this step today, it is a first step. It can't restore the bonds of trust by itself. It can't restore the sense of understanding that is necessary for people to live together. So I will also acknowledge that success depends not only on what you say or sign in Arusha, also what you do in the weeks and months and years ahead in Burundi. The agreements you reach have to be respected and implemented both in letter and spirit. Again, I say, if you decide to do this, everyone must acknowledge there must be no victors and no vanquished. If one side feels defeated, it will be likely to fight again, and no Burundian will be secure. And, after all, security for all is one of the main arguments for doing this.

Now, let me say something else. Of course, you must confront the past with honesty. There is hardly a Burundian family that has not felt the sorrow of losing a loved one to violence. The history must be told, the causes must be understood. Those responsible for violence against innocent people must be held accountable. But what is the goal here? The goal must be to end the cycle of violence, not perpetuate it.

So I plead with you; I've seen this a lot of places, and it's always the same. You have to help your children remember their history, but you must not force them to relive their history. They deserve to live in their tomorrows, not in your yesterdays. Let me just make one other point. When all is said and done, only you can bring an end to the bloodshed and sorrow your country has suffered. Nelson Mandela will be a force for peace. The United States will try to be a force for peace. But no one can force peace; you must choose it. Now, again, I say, I watched the parties in Ireland fight for 30 years. I've watched the parties in the Middle East fight for 50 years. I've watched the parties in the Balkans now go at it and then quit and then go at it again, and then I've watched — saw a million people driven out of Kosovo. And when we began to talk about peace in Bosnia, the three different ethnic and religious groups didn't even want to sit down together in the same room.

But when it's all said and done, it always comes down to the same thing. You have to find a way to support democracy and respect for the majority, and their desires. You have to have minority rights, including security. You have to have shared decision-making, and there must be shared benefits from your living together.

Now, you can walk away from all this and fight some more and worry about it, and let somebody come back here 10 years from now. No matter how long you take, when it comes down to it, they'll still be dealing with the same issues. And I say, if you let anybody else die because you can't bring this together now, all you will do is make it harder for people to make the same decisions you're going to have to make here anyway.

So I will say again: If you decide, if you choose, not because anybody is forcing you, but because you know it is right to give your children their tomorrows; if you choose peace, the United States and the world community will be there to help you make it pay off. We will strongly support an appropriate role for the U.N. in helping to implement it. We will support your efforts to demobilize combatants and to integrate them into a national army.

We will help you bring refugees home and to meet the needs of displaced children and orphans. We will help you to create the economic and social conditions essential to a sustainable peace — from agricultural development to child immunization, to the prevention of AIDS. I know this is hard, but I believe you can do it. Consider the case of Mozambique. A civil war there took a million lives, most of them innocent civilians. Of every five infants born in Mozambique during the civil war, three — three — died before their fifth birthday, either murdered or stricken by disease.

Those who survived grew up knowing nothing but war. Yet today, Mozambique is at peace. It has found a way to include everyone in its political life, and out of the devastation. Last year it had one of the five fastest-growing economies in the entire world. Now, you can do that. But you have to choose. And you have to decide if you're going to embrace that. You have to create a lot of room in your mind and heart and spirit for that kind of future. So you have to let some things go.

Now, Mr. Mandela — he's the world's greatest example of letting things go. But when we got to be friends, I said to him one day, in a friendly way, I said, you know, Mandela, you're a great friend, but you're also a great politician. It was quite smart to invite your jailers to your inauguration. Good politics. But tell me the truth, now. When they let you out of jail the last time and you were walking to freedom, didn't you have a moment when you were really, really angry at them again? You know what he said? He said, yes, I did — a moment. Then I realized I had been in prison for 27 years, and if I hated them after I got out, I would still be their prisoner, and I wanted to be free.

Sooner or later, hatred, vengeance, the illusion that power over another group of people will bring security in life, these feelings can be just as iron, just as confining as the doors of a prison cell. I don't ask you to forget what you went through in the bitter years. But I hope you will go home to Burundi not as prisoners of the past, but builders of the future. I will say again, if you decide, America and the world will be with you. but you, and only you, must decide whether to give your children their own tomorrows.

Thank you very much.

Remarks by President Clinton
At the Congressional Black Caucus Foundation Dinner
Washington Convention Center
Washington, D.C.

September 16, 2000

Thank you very much, Chairman Clyburn; dinner Chair Eddie Bernice Johnson, my friend of 28 years — and didn't she give a great introduction to the Vice President. You better go on the road, girl. Our foundation chair, Eva Clayton and all the members and former members of the CBC, especially to my friend, Bill Clay. We wish you well and godspeed on your retirement, and I thank you for eight years of our good partnership.

To Mrs. Coretta Scott King and all the distinguished citizens in the audience, but especially to the two whom I had the great honor to award the Presidential Medal of Freedom, Marian Wright Edelman and Reverend Jesse Jackson, thank you for being here with us tonight.

I thank Lou Stokes and Phylicia Rashad and want to join in congratulating the award winners, my friend, Arthur Eve, whose son did such a good job working for the Clinton-Gore administration. Kenneth Hill, Rodney Carroll, who has been great on our Welfare To Work program. Tom Joyner, who lets me jaw on his radio program from time to time. Even I never got an eight-page spread in Ebony; I don't know about that.

To Tavis Smiley and to the family of our friend, LeBaron Taylor, Bill Kennard, and Ambassador Sisulu, thank you for what you said about our friend, Nelson Mandela. I thank Attorney General Reno and Secretary Slater and Secretary Herman and Deputy Attorney General Holder and our SBA Director, Aida Alvarez, and all the people from our White House team who are here, and from the entire administration.

I thought the Vice President gave a great speech, and I'm looking forward to getting rid of that trouble adjective at the beginning of his title in just a couple of months now.

Now, there was nothing subliminal about that. We Democrats don't have subliminal advertising. I also want to thank Senator Lieberman, who has been a friend since Hillary and I met him 30 years ago when he was running for the state senate in New Haven. And I can tell you that if he is the vice president of this country, you will be very, very proud of him. He has done a great job, and he has been a great friend of mine.

I want to bring you a warm welcome from Hillary. She wishes she could be here tonight, but she's otherwise occupied. They sent the one in our family who is not running for office this year to speak to you tonight.

I've been honored to be at every one of these dinners since I became President. Tonight, I came mostly to listen and to clap, and to say thanks. Thank you for your friendship, your leadership and your support. Thank you for giving me the chance, John Lewis, to walk with you in Selma this year. Thank you, for those of you who went back to Africa with me when we went to Nigeria and Tanzania. Thank you for working with me to reach out to the people of Africa and the Caribbean, to try to build their countries through trade.

Thank you, for those of you who helped me to relieve the debt of the poor countries and to increase our fight against AIDS and TB and malaria around the world.

The Vice President said that there are so many people who could say that the CBC covered their back. Covered their back? (Laughter.) When they took a torch to me and lit the fire, you brought the buckets and poured the water on it. And I thank you. Thank you. (Applause.)

But mostly, I want to thank you for taking our nation to higher ground, for standing with Al Gore and me in our simple, but profound mission to make sure that everyone counts and everyone has a chance, to make sure that we act as if we all do better when we help each other.

I can't thank you enough for your role in all the good things that have happened in the last eight years. It's all been recited. I guess what I would like for you to know is that there are a lot of days when I just felt like the troubadour, but other people had to play in the orchestra and even write the songs. And nothing — nothing good that I have achieved would have been possible without the Congressional Black Caucus, our other friends in Congress, and especially Vice President Al Gore. And I thank you all for that.

I just want to say two serious things about the future tonight. The first is, that when Al Gore says you ain't seen nothing' yet, I agree with him. We've spent a lot of time in the last eight years trying to turn this country around and get it together and get it moving in the right direction. And now, for the first time in our lifetime, we have both prosperity and the absence of serious internal crisis and external threat.

We actually can build the future of our dreams for our kids. We could get rid of child poverty. We could give every child in America the chance at a world-class education for the first time. We could open the doors of college to all. We could take Social Security and Medicare out there beyond the life of the baby boomers and add that prescription drug benefit.

We could do a lot of things with these unbelievable discoveries in science and technology. But we have to make a decision. And so the second point I want to make is, sometimes it's harder to make a good decision in good times than bad times. I know the people took a chance on me in 1992 but, give me a break, the country was in a ditch; it wasn't that much of a chance.

I mean, you know, they — I don't know how many voters went into the polling place and thought, you know, I don't know if I want to vote for that guy. He's a governor — President Bush said he was the governor of a small southern state and I don't even know where that place is on the map and he looks too young and everybody says he's terrible. But we had to change.

Now things are going well and people are comfortable and confident and we have options. So it's up to you to make sure that people ask the right question and answer it in this election season. That we say we cannot afford to pass up the chance of a lifetime, maybe the chance of a half a century, to build the future of our dreams for our children.

And there is a lot at stake. You've heard it all tonight, just about, how we're fighting for strong schools and modern classrooms and a higher minimum wage and all the other things. I would like to mention one other thing that hasn't been talked about. We ought to be fighting for an end to delay and discrimination against highly qualified minority candidates for the federal courts.

This Administration has named 62 African-American judges, three times the number of the previous two administrations combined, with the highest ratings from the ABA in 40 years. Yet, we know, in spite of that, that women and minority candidates are still much more likely to be delayed or denied.

So even though this is a non-profit organization, I can ask you to remember Judge Ronnie White, the first African American on the Missouri Supreme Court, denied on the party line vote. The Fourth Circuit with the largest African American population in the country never had an African American judge. Last year, I told you I nominated James Wynn, a distinguished judge from North Carolina. After 400 days, with his senior senator still standing in the courthouse door, the Senate hasn't found one day to give Judge Wynn even a hearing.

This year, I nominated Roger Gregory of Virginia, the first man in his family to finish high school, a teacher at Virginia State University, where his mother once worked as a maid, a highly respected litigator with the support of his Republican and his Democratic senator from Virginia. But, so far, we're still waiting for him to get a hearing. And then there's Kathleen McCree Lewis in Michigan and others all across this country.

So once again, I ask the Senate to do the right thing and quit closing the door on people who are qualified to serve.

Now, they say I can't ask you to vote for anybody but I will say this. If you want no more delay and denial of justice, it would help if you had Al Gore and Joe Lieberman and senators like the First Lady.

If you want a tax code that helps working families with child care, long-term care and access to college education, it would help if you had Al Gore and Joe Lieberman and Charlie Rangel as the Chairman of the House Ways and Means Committee.

If you want strong civil rights and equal rights laws and you want them enforced, it would really help if you had Al Gore and Joe Lieberman and you made John Conyers the Chairman of the Judiciary Committee.

If you want the intelligence policy of this country to reflect genuine intelligence — it would help if you had Al Gore and Joe Lieberman and Julian Dixon as the Chairman of the Intelligence Committee.

But I will say again, sometimes it is harder to make good decisions in good times than bad times. Sometimes it's easier to think of some little thing you've got to quibble about. Remember the African proverb: "Smooth seas do not make skillful sailors." My friends, we've got to be skillful sailors.

I thank you from the bottom of my heart. Toni Morrison once said I was the first black President this country ever had. And I would rather have that than a Nobel Prize. And I'll tell you why. Because somewhere, in the deep and lost threads of my own memory are the roots of understanding of what you have known. Somewhere, there was a deep longing to share the fate of the people who had been left out and left behind, sometimes brutalized and too often ignored or forgotten.

I don't exactly know who all I have to thank for that. But I'm quite sure I don't deserve any credit for it. Because whatever I did, I would have felt I had no other choice.

I want you to remember that I had a partner that felt the same way, that I believe he will be one of the great presidents this country ever had and that, for the rest of my days, no matter what, no matter what, I will always be there for you.

Thank you and God bless you.

Remarks by President Clinton at the Entebbe Summit for Peace and Prosperity
Imperial Botanical Beach Hotel
Entebbe, Uganda

March 25, 1998

President Museveni, President Moi, Prime Minister Meles, President Bizimungu, President Mkapa, President Kabila, Secretary General Salim; to our distinguished guests, all. Let me, first of all, thank the representatives of all the governments who are here, and the leaders who have come to Entebbe to share a common vision of a brighter future for this region.

We seek to deepen the progress that has been made and to meet the tough challenges that remain. We came to Entebbe because we share a commitment to strengthen our cooperation, to build a partnership for the 21st century that will benefit all our people.

We understand, and the last statement I made at our meeting was that these goals will not be met in one meeting or one day or one year, but we have formed a solid foundation for progress in the future. Our challenge as we leave Entebbe is to bring to life the commitment in the remarkable document we have just signed.

What is in the document? First, we have agreed to deepen our efforts to promote democracy and respect for human rights, the precious soil in which peace and prosperity grow. When men and women alike are treated with dignity, when they have a say in decisions that affect their lives, societies are better equipped to seize the opportunities of the future.

We have emphasized the importance of freely elected, accountable governments; affirmed the vital role of civic organizations in building strong and vibrant societies; and pledged to uphold humanitarian principles, including the protection and care of refugees.

America knows from our own experience that there is no single blueprint for a successful democracy. We're still working in our country to create what our founders called a more perfect union. We've been at it for 222 years now. But we also know that while there is no single blueprint, freedom, nonetheless, is a universal aspiration. Human rights are not bestowed on the basis of wealth or race, of gender or ethnicity, of culture or region. They are the birthright of all men and women everywhere.

If we work together to strengthen democracy and respect human rights, we can help this continent reach its full potential in the 21st century — its true greatness, which has too long been denied. We can deepen the ties among our peoples. We can be a force for good together, and all our nations can be proud.

Second, we have agreed to work together to build a new economic future, where the talents of Africa's people are unleashed, the doors of opportunity are opened to all, and countries move from the margins to the mainstream of the global economy. We committed to work on finding new strategies to hasten Africa's global integration. We pledged to speed the regional cooperation that is already underway, to encourage common standards for openness and anti-corruption, to continue to be responsive to the burden of debt.

A key part of our effort is expanding the ties of trade and investment between our countries so that African development and Asian growth — and American growth, excuse me — reinforce one another. We want to reward each other for working together. Before I left for Africa I told the American people that it was in our interest to help Africa grow and blossom and reach its full potential. I believe that.

I want to thank the members of the United States House of Representatives who are on this trip with me for their leadership in the passage in the House of the African Growth and Opportunity Act. I am committed to the swift passage of that act in the United State Senate and to signing it when I return home. I am very pleased that our Overseas Private Investment Corporation will be targeting half a billion dollars for infrastructure investment in sub-Saharan Africa.

Third, we have agreed to work together to banish genocide from this region and this continent. Every African child has the right to grow up in safety and peace. We condemn the perpetrators of the continued atrocities in Rwanda, and pledge to work together to end the horrors of this region. That means reviving the U.N. Arms Flow Commission, acting on the recommendations of the OAU study on the Rwandan genocide and its aftermath; encouraging accelerated progress in bringing criminals against humanity to justice; denying safe havens or services to extremist organizations; and developing durable justice systems that are credible, impartial, and effective. Our efforts come too late for yesterday's victims. They must be in time to prevent tomorrow's victims.

Here today — and this is very important — we have pledged to find new ways to work together to solve conflicts before they explode into crises and to act to stop them more quickly when they do.

We have pursued our discussion in a spirit of candor and mutual respect, and I want to thank all the participants for being honest and open in our conversations. America shares a stake in Africa's success, as I said. If African nations become stronger, as they surely will, if they become more dynamic, as they clearly are, we can become even better partners in meeting our common challenges. Your stability, your security, your prosperity will add to our own. And our vitality can and must contribute to yours.

I've learned a lot here in Entebbe today, listening — and will carry back to Washington, as I'm sure the rest of our delegation will. We've agreed to build on this summit with regular, high-level meetings. We will look for results of our efforts not only in statements like this one today, with very high visibility, but in quiet places far from the halls of government; in communities and households all across our countries, where ordinary men and women strive each day to build strong families, to find good jobs, to pass on better lives for their children. They are the reason we are here. And it is because of them that we all leave Entebbe determined to put our partnership into practice, to make our dreams and ideals real.

Remarks by President Clinton at Goree Island
Goree Island, Senegal

April 2, 1998

Thank you, Mr. President, for that magnificent address. Thank you so much. Now, all my friends will have to tell me if the translation is working. Yes, it's working? Hurray!

Mr. President, Madame Diouf, the ministers and officials of the Senegalese government, Governor, Mayor; to the students who are here who have sung to us and with whom we have met from the Martin Luther King School, the John F. Kennedy School — the Miriama Ba School here on Goree Island — and the Margaret Amidon Elementary School in Washington, D.C. — the residents of Goree Island, the citizens of Senegal — my fellow Americans and our delegation, ladies and gentlemen.

I'd also like to say a special word of thanks to the curator, Bubaka Ndiaye, who toured me through the slave house today. Thank you, sir. Here, on this tiny island in the Atlantic Ocean, Africa and America meet. From here, Africa expands to the east; its potential for freedom and progress as great as its landmass. And to the west, over the horizon, lies America — a thriving democracy built, as President Diouf said, through centuries of sacrifice.

Long after the slave ships stopped sailing from this place to America, Goree Island, still today, looks out onto the New World, connecting two continents, standing as a vivid reminder that for some of America's ancestors the journey to America was anything but a search for freedom; and yet still, a symbol of the bright new era of partnership between our peoples.

In 1776, when our nation was founded on the promise of freedom as God's right to all human beings, a new building was dedicated here on Goree Island to the selling of human beings in bondage to America. Goree Island is, therefore, as much a part of our history as a part of Africa's history. From Goree and other places, Africa's sons and daughters were taken through the door of no return, never to see their friends and family again.

Those who survived the murderous middle passage emerged from a dark hold to find themselves, yes, American. But it would be a long, long time before their descendants enjoyed the full meaning of that word. We cannot push time backward through the door of no return. We have lived our history. America's struggle to overcome slavery and its legacy forms one of the most difficult chapters of that history. Yet, it is also one of the most heroic; a triumphant of courage, persistence, and dignity. The long journey of African Americans proves that the spirit can never be enslaved. And that long journey is today embodied by the children of Africa who now lead America, in all phases of our common life. Many of them have come here with me on this visit, representing over 30 million Americans that are Africa's great gift to America. And I'd like them to stand now. Please stand.

A few hours from now, we will leave Africa and go on home, back to the work of building our own country for a new century. But I return more convinced than when I came here that despite the daunting challenges, there is an African renaissance.

I will never forget as long as I live the many faces that Hillary and I have seen in these last 12 days. In them, I have seen beauty and intelligence — energy and spirit, and the determination to prevail. I have seen the faces of Africa's future. The friendly faces of the hundreds of thousands of people who poured into Independence Square in Accra to show that Africans feel warmly toward America.

The faces of the children at the primary school in Uganda, whose parents were held back by a brutal dictatorship, but where today opportunity of education is offered to all of that nation's boys and girls. The faces of the women in Wanyange Village in Uganda, once ordained to a life of continuing struggle, now empowered, along with 10,000 other Ugandans and women and men in Senegal and virtually every other country in Africa by microcredit loans to start their own businesses, small loans which people repay and which repay them by giving them the opportunity to live a better life.

I will always remember the faces of the survivors of the Rwandan genocide, who have the courage now not just to survive, but to build a better society. I will never forget the face of Nelson Mandela in his cell on Robin Island — a face that betrays a spirit not broken, but strengthened; not embittered, but energized; a man used his suffering to break the shackles of apartheid, and now to reach toward reconciliation.

I remember the faces of the young leaders I have met — young leaders of the new South Africa; young leaders who want to build a continent where the economy grows, but where the environment is preserved and your vast riches that nature has bestowed are no longer depleted; young leaders who believe that Africa can go forward as a free, free continent, where people, all people, enjoy universal human rights. I remember their faces so well.

I remember the faces of the entrepreneurs, African and American, who gathered with me in Johannesburg to dedicate Ron Brown Commercial Center. I thank you, Mr. President, for mentioning our friend, Ron Brown — for it was he who first told me that I had an obligation as an American President to build a better partnership with Africa.

Already, we import about as much oil from Africa as we do from the Persian Gulf. We export more to Africa than to all the former Soviet Union. And Americans should know that our investments in sub-Saharan Africa are in a return of 30 percent, higher than on any other continent in the entire world. But our trade and investment in Africa is but a tiny fraction of what it could be, and, therefore, of what it could produce — in new jobs, new opportunities, new wealth, and new dreams for Africans and for Americans. The faces I saw will spur us to do better.

Mr. President, I remember the faces of the Senegalese soldiers yesterday, whom we saw training with Americans, but led by Africans in an African Crisis Response Initiative dedicated to the prevention of violence, to the relief of suffering, to keeping the peace on the continent of Africa. Most of all, I will always remember in every country the faces of the little children — the beautiful children — the light in their eyes, the smiles on their faces, the songs that they sung. We owe it to them, you and I, to give them the best possible future they can have.

Yes, Africa still faces poverty, malnutrition, disease, illiteracy, unemployment, terrible conflicts in some places. In some countries, human rights are still nonexistent and unevenly respected in others. But look across the continent. Democracy is gaining strength. Business is growing. Peace is making progress. The people and the leaders of Africa are showing the world the resiliency of the human spirit and the future of this great continent.

They have convinced me of the difference America can make if we are a genuine partner and friend of Africa, and the difference a new Africa can make to America's own future. Everywhere I went in Africa I saw a passionate belief in the promise of America, stated more eloquently today by your President than I ever could.

I only wish every American could see our own country as so much of Africa sees us — a nation bearing the ideals of freedom and equality and responsible citizenship, so powerful they still light the world; a nation that has found strength in our racial and ethnic and religious diversity; a nation, therefore, that must lead by the power of example; a nation that stands for what so many aspire to and now are achieving, the freedom to dream dreams and the opportunity to make those dreams come true.

I am very proud of America's ties to Africa, for there is no area of American achievement that has not been touched by the intelligence and energy of Africa — from science to medicine, to literature, to art, to music. I am proud to be the President of a nation of many colors, black and white, European and Latino, Asian and Middle Eastern and everything in between.

We have learned one clear lesson, that when we embrace one another across the lines that divide us, we become more than the sum of our parts, a community of communities, a nation of nations. Together, we work to face the future as one America — undaunted, undivided, grateful for the chance to live together as one people.

To be sure, our work is not finished and we have our own problems. But when we began as a nation, our founders knew that, and called us always to the work of forming a more perfect union. But the future before us expands as wide as the ocean that joins, not divides, the United States and Africa. As certainly as America lies over the horizon behind me, so I pledge to the people of Africa that we will reach over this ocean to build a new partnership based on friendship and respect.

As we leave this island now is the time to complete the circle of history, to help Africa to fulfill its promise not only as a land of rich beauty, but as a land of rich opportunity for all its people. If we face the future together it will be a future that is better for Africa and better for America. So we leave Goree Island today mindful of the large job still to be done, proud of how far we have come, proud of how far Africa has come; determined to succeed in building a bright, common destiny whose door is open to all.

Thank you and God bless you.

Remarks by President Clinton at the Signing of the Trade and Development Act of 2000
South Lawn
The White House

May 18, 2000

I would like to, first of all, welcome all of you here, to the South Lawn, on this beautiful day for this important occasion. I thank the members of the Cabinet and the administration who are here.

I thank the very large number of members of Congress who are here from both parties, the mayors and other public officials who supported this legislation. I want to thank our Special Envoy for the Americas, Buddy MacKay, my point person on the Caribbean Basin Initiative; and our former and first Special Envoy to the Americas, Mack McLarty.

I'd like to say a special word of appreciation to Senator Roth and Senator Moynihan; to Representative Rangel and Representative Archer; to Senator Lott and to Speaker Hastert, who supported this legislation; and to all the members who worked so hard to get this bill passed, including Representatives Crane, Jefferson, McDermott, Payne, Royce, and so many others who are here, too numerous to mention. I want to thank the members of the Diplomatic Corps who are here, who also supported this initiative.

The votes in the House and the Senate for the Trade and Development Act of 2000, what is commonly known as Africa-CBI, were bipartisan and overwhelming, because they reflect the judgment that the results of this legislation will be good for the United States, good for Africa, good for Central America, and the Caribbean.

This day has been a long time coming. But it is here. It is clear that by breaking down barriers to trade, building new opportunities and raising prosperity, we can lift lives in every country and on every continent. Nowhere is that more apparent than here in the United States, where our exports and our open markets have given us the longest expansion in our history, with low inflation.

This bill reaffirms that position. And I hope it will be reaffirmed next week, when Congress votes on permanent normal trade relations with China. Congress will have another opportunity in considering the Trade Preference Act for the Balkans, another poor region of the world that is important to our future.

Today, I want to focus, though, on the areas that are affected by this legislation — on the Caribbean Basin and Africa.

Sub-Saharan Africa is home to more than 700 million people, one of our biggest potential trade partners. I say "potential" because American exports now account for only six percent of the African market. This bill will surely change that as it expands Africa's access to our markets and improves the ability of African nations to ease poverty, increase growth and heal the problems of their people. It promotes the kinds of economic reform that will make sub-Saharan nations, in the long run, better allies, better trade partners and stronger nations.

Closer to home, in the Caribbean Basin, we already have strong trade relations. Last year, our exports to the region exceeded $19 billion, making it the sixth largest market for our goods — larger than France or Brazil. That is remarkable, but not as remarkable as the transformation of Central America and the Caribbean as a whole.

Despite the aftermath of war, the devastation of natural disasters, the region has made great strides toward recovery, democracy, peace and prosperity. On all my visits to the region, I have marveled at these changes.

Trade is one of the most powerful engines driving development in the region, and the Caribbean Basin Initiative has played a part. It's a key building block to a free trade area of the Americas, which I hope we will have in the next few years.

What we see in the Caribbean Basin and in Africa is that trade can broaden the benefits of the global economy and lift the lives of people everywhere. But it is not enough, and our agenda for the developing world must be multifaceted, recognizing that trade must work for all people, and that spirited competition should lift all nations. I am pleased, for example, that this bill contains important child labor protections, authored by Senator Harkin.

I'd also like to say that there's another big issue I hope we'll take up, as the Congress had been willing to do last year, and again in a bipartisan fashion — too many nations, developing nations, are still forced to choose between paying interest on their debts and meeting basic human needs for clean water, shelter, health and education. Last year, the wealthiest nations pledged faster and deeper debt relief to developing nations that make needed reforms — countries like Honduras, Nicaragua, many in sub-Saharan Africa. In September, I pledged to go even further and make it possible to forgive all the debt of the poorest countries — that the poorest countries owe to the United States. And I am pleased that since then — since then, every other wealthy nation has made the same commitment.

Now, we're here today because so many members of Congress and those who talk to them dedicated themselves to trade, to development, to the future of the Caribbean Basin and Africa. Today, I ask that we apply that same energy to our debt relief efforts.

I would also just like to take a few moments to remind you of what we all know, which is that there are enormous health challenges in the developing nations, which threaten their prosperity, their future, and could threaten their democracy. We know the massive human and economic costs the AIDS epidemic exacts in Africa, where every day 5,500 people die.

Last week, I took executive action, building on the work of Senator Feinstein, to make AIDS-related drugs more affordable there. I've asked the Congress to enact tax incentives to speed the development and delivery of vaccines for AIDS, malaria and tuberculosis, and to contribute to a global fund for the purchase of such vaccines so that they will go where they're most needed. And I hope again we will have a strong bipartisan level of support for this.

Finally, let me say that the legislation I sign today is about more than development and trade. It's about transforming our relationship with two regions full of good people trying to build good futures who are very important to our own future.

During the Cold War, to many Americans, Central America was a battleground and Africa was a backwater. All that has changed. We have worked hard the last few years to build genuine partnership with both regions — based on not what we can do for them, not what we can do about them, but on what we can do with them to build democracy together.

Let me finally say just a couple of words about Africa, because the good news this week comes against the backdrop of some tragic developments on the continent. Two of Africa's poorest, but most promising nations — Ethiopia and Eritrea — resumed their senseless war. For over two years we've worked with the OAU to resolve that dispute. We won't abandon the effort. But Ethiopia and Eritrea must first see that backing away from self-destruction is not the same thing as backing down. Giving your people a future is not cowardice, it's common sense and courage.

We are also working with our African partners to support the people of Sierra Leone and the U.N. forces there, and we will do what is necessary to provide military transport and other support so the U.N. will get the reinforcement it needs.

We need to see the problems of Africa plainly and do our best to meet them. But that must not obscure the promise of Africa, which is also profoundly clear. It is the home to three of the world's fastest economies — three of the four fastest growing economies in the world are African economies. The progress of democracy, from Nigeria to South Africa; the proof offered by countries like Uganda that AIDS and other diseases can be arrested and the rates can be reduced, where the governments care to try and work with people to do the hard things. Even in Sierra Leone, we see signs of hope, and we have been working with other nations in Africa to increase the capacity to meet the challenge there.

We must not avoid our neighbors in Central America and the Caribbean, or our friends half a world away in Africa. We must build a better future together with both. That's what this is all about. That's the ultimate message of this trade bill.

I could not be prouder that over 70 percent of both Houses voted for this legislation; that majorities in both parties supported this legislation.

Again, Mr. Speaker, I want to thank you and Senator Lott for the role you played. I want to thank the members of the Congressional Black Caucus and the Hispanic Caucus and the others whom I have just mentioned, and everyone else who is here. This is a happy day for America. And five years from now, 10 years from now, 15 years from now, as we grow closer and closer and closer to our neighbors in the Caribbean and Central America, and to our friends in Africa, we will look back on this day and say this was a big part of how it all began.

Thank you very much.

And now I'd like to call up here a gentleman who worked very, very hard for this day: the Minority Leader of the Democrats on the House Ways and Means Committee, Mr. Charles Rangel from New York.

I would like to invite all the members of Congress who are here to please come up and join us on the stage for the signing, along with Ambassador MacKay, wherever he is. Come on up here.

(The bill is signed.)

acknowledgments

We thank God for the vision.

We owe a deep debt of gratitude to many whose contributions enhanced this work.

We thank our diverse and distinguished Board of Directors, all of whom supported this endeavor from conception through publication.

Our most sincere thanks go to our Chairman, Alhaji Bamanga Tukur, whose vision and motivation inspired us to produce this book. Board member Samuel Dossou, former Chairman of OPIC Board of Governors and Chairman of Petrolink UK LTD, a Geneva-based firm specializing in petroleum, whose vision for ACA is that it becomes a viable company that brings together the best of both worlds.

Board member Dr. Babacar Ndiaye, Ambassador-at-Large from Senegal and former President of the African Development Bank, who constantly reminded us that "Africa is a place of hope, a place of opportunity, a place of high return on investment. We are talking about 600-700 million people in more than 40 countries who are aspiring for a better life, who are on the right course of democratization."

Dr. Khalid Abdullah Tariq Al-Mansour, an international lawyer and scholar, noted, "We need that [racial pride] to inspire our children to attain excellence in education and in business. It's the same with the Jews, the Chinese, and the Japanese. They started off with racial pride. That's what gave them their unity and solidarity. It gave them the discipline. If Africa, first of all, is not recognized by African Americans, and if, second, we are not moving Africa forward, then one has reduced the prospect of racial pride."

Charlette Neighbors, an ACA founding member, is one of several African Americans who sit on ACA's Board. Her media sales and programming experience span more than 30 years, and she has traveled extensively throughout Africa. The recipient of several prestigious awards, Neighbors feels it is important that African Americans work together to create a good African image. "Africa is our motherland and we have to understand that the elevation of Africa is the elevation of all of us."

ACA's Chief Executive Officer, Abdul Latif Bennett, a 36-year-old African American has found tremendous rewards in serving Africa and its people and considers his position to be more as a calling than a job.

We thank President Clinton for America's new thinking on Africa and look forward to building bridges of healing, partnership and innovation to ensure that all future chapters in U.S.-Africa relations glorify our ancestors and Africans on both sides of the Atlantic.

We also thank the ACAP team. Their vision, commitment, and hard work are revealed in each of the pages you have read. They are: Abdul Latif Bennett (Chief Executive Officer), Anita Omitowoju (Vice President of Marketing), Victoria Ogun (Director of Marketing), Tony Regusters (Video Producer/Public Relations Consultant/Journalist), and Yemi Etta (Project Manager).

Others deserving our gratitude include: Yvette Reyes of AP Worldwide Photos who often provided research and technical assistance; Joyce Gowie Gamble, ACA's computer specialist; Jarrin Davis and Daniel Olds of Zebra Designs, Inc., for their unwavering creativity and professionalism; and Jean Bernard and Lurma Rackley for their proofreading and editing expertise.

We extend a special thanks to Sharolyn Rosier Hyson's parents, James and Vivian Rosier, for instilling a love and respect for our history and to her husband, Greg Hyson, who supported her through the long hours of work with no dinner in sight, often reading pages before anyone else.

Thanks go as well to our friends and advisors: Dr. Ada Adler, Musa Aduak, The African Magazine, Dr. Agary, Alhaji and Mrs. Al-Hassan, Noah Aremu, Kola Aremu, Obi Atuyana, Dr. Peter Balagon, Bernice Barber, Brenda Belton, Erie and Dessaree Bennett, Larry Bennett, Mrs. Lewistein Bennett, Marion Bennett, Miecha L. Bennett, Timothy Bork, Betty Bridges, Evelyn Brown, Mrs. Inez Bryant, Erie Chinje, Mr. and Mrs. John Clark, Mahar Alexander Bennington Cooke, Marleene Cox, Alice Dear, Maureen Dailey, George Darden, Steven Davenport, Ambassador and Mrs. Joseph Diatta, Karimah Dillard, Duncan Dokowari, Ivory Dorsey, Jevie Dumas, Selma Edwards, Braks Etta, Nate Fields, Mel Foote, Senator Robert Ford, Professor Ibrahim Gambari, Professor Jerry Gana, Obi Gbadebo, Yvonne Green, Joan Guiraras, Congressman Alcee Hastings, The Hebrew Israelites, Adonis Hoffman, Mazie Holland, Sanford Holloway, Cathy Hughes, Betty Hyman, The Hyson Family, Alhaji Isyaku Ibrahim, Chief Bola Ige, Eartha Jackson, Ethel Jackson, Jackie Jackson, Zainab M. Jaji, Dr. Sidi Jammeh, Susan Johnson, Marvin Jones, Thelma Jones, Grace Keboh, Lynne Kraselsky, General and Mrs. Fred Leigh, Dr. Toni Luck, C. Payne Lucas, Mike Luke, Saundra Magana, Marvin MaGraw, Tappy Malloy, Judy Mapondera, Katie Mapondera, General B. Marwa, Ann McNeil, Sister Claudette Muhammad, Lota Mushaw, The Nation of Islam, Professor Bart Nnaji, James Obi, Dr. A'Jowan, Dr. Doyin O'Kupe, Ade Omitowoju, Desmond Orage, Aunt Ida Owens, Johan Owens, Jon Owens, Lauri Fitz Pegado, The Perry Center, H.E. Ruth Perry, Luke Range, Cynthia Reid, James D. Rosier, Nicole Salifa, Soumanou Salifa Daisy Saunders, Freddie and Tina Savage, Ambassador Mamadou Seck, Nakia Simms, Gregory B. Simpkins, Archbishop George Stallings, Herb Straughters, Dr. Niara Sudarkasa, Chairman Percy Sutton, Lionel Terrell, Professor Babatunde Thomas, Nardos

Thomas, Dr. Darleen Thompson, Jackie Thredgill, Thell Torrence, The Tukur Family, Linda Wadsworth, The Walker Family, Dr. Christine Wanky, Catherine Weedon, Rosa Whitaker, Mike Williams, Terri Williams, Larry Wize, Darleen Woods.

Last but not least, we thank people who provided help and encouragement in so many ways — Kayode Soyinka, publisher of *Africa Today;* Soumanou Salifou, publisher of *The African*; Rick Johnson, cameraman; Art Thomas, cameraman; the Federal Republic of Nigeria, the Office of the President and the Ministry of Information; the Embassies of Ghana, Senegal, and Uganda; Karen Craun and Becky Moore of RR Donnelly & Sons Company; Kathleen Hughes of Capital Books, Ruth Cooke Gibbs of Ruder Finn; Sharon Farmer, Maureen Hudson, Janis Kearney, and Kirsten Wilson of the White House; Rosa Whitaker, the Office of the U.S. Trade Representative; Vivian Lowery-Derryck and Dr. Sarah Moten of the U.S. Agency for International Development, Ernest G. Green, chairman of the African Development Bank and managing director of Public Finance for Lehman Brothers' Washington, D.C. office.

We also thank the following organizations for their continual support of Africa: the Bridge International Group; the African Business Roundtable; The United Nations; The United Nations Foundation; the World Bank Africa Club; Constituency for Africa; Africare; USAID; International Foundation for Education and Self Help; Citizens International; Modern African Fund Managers; New Africa Advisors; the African American Institute; the Global Coalition for Africa; the National Summit on Africa; Carnegie Endowment for International Peace; Healthcare International Management Company; Goodworks International; Worldspace Corporation; Corporate Council on Africa; and TransAfrica.

Sources

Promoting Peace and Democracy

1994 Presidential Documents Online via GPO Access, www.gpo.gov, Volume 30—Number 26, Pages 1351-1395

The White House, www.whitehouse.gov/africa
- Fact Sheet, Background to the Burundi Peace Process, February 22, 2000
- Remarks by the President in Address at Burundi Peace Talks, August 28, 2000
- Remarks by the President at the Entebbe Summit for Peace and Prosperity, March 25, 1998
- Entebbe Summit for Peace and Prosperity, Joint Declaration of Principles, March 25 1998
- Remarks by President Clinton to Genocide Survivors, March 25, 1998
- Fact Sheet, Countering Genocide and Promoting Human Rights, March 26, 1998
- President Clinton: Supporting Human Rights in Africa and Around the World, September 23, 1998
- Fact Sheet, Initiatives with Ghana, March 28, 1998
- Statement by President Clinton on Deportation of Liberians and Memorandum for the Attorney
- General on Certain Liberians in the U.S., September 28, 2000
- Statement by the Press Secretary, Radio Democracy for Africa, March 29, 1998

U.S. Department of State, African Crisis Response Initiative (ACRI) Fact Sheet, August 31, 2000

U.S. Department of Defense, Office of the Assistant Secretary of Defense (Public Affairs), DOD
- Launches African Center for Strategic Studies, July 22, 1999, Press Release No. 343-99

U.S. Agency for International Development
- Greater Horn of Africa Initiative: Executive Summary, www.usaid.gov/regions/afr/ghai/cycle/execsumm.html
- Great Lakes Initiative, www.usaid.gov/democracy/afr/gli.html
- Democracy Program, www.usaid.gov/democracy/afr/nigeriaso.html
- Initiative for Southern Africa, www.usaid.gov/democracy/afr/isa.html
- Building Democracy in Ghana, www.usaid.gov/democracy/afr/ghana.html
- Democracy Program: Liberia, www.usaid.gov/democracy/afr/liberiaso.html

The Federal Republic of Nigeria, Ministry of Information and National Orientation, "President Bill Clinton's Visit to Nigeria."

Fostering Trade and Economic Development

The White House, www.whitehouse.gov/africa
- Fact Sheet, Ron Brown Commercial Center, March 28, 1998
- Remarks by the President at the Ron Brown Commercial Center, March 28, 1998

Details of the Trade and Development Act of 2000, May 17, 2000
Statement by the President on the Signing of the Foreign Operations, Export Financing, and Related Programs, November 6, 2000

U.S. Department of State
- U.S.-South Africa Binational Commission, www.state.gov
- U.S. Government Initiatives for Africa

U.S. Department of Transportation
- Safe Skies for Africa, www.dot.gov
- U.S. Department of Transportation Initiative and Partnership with Africa (Transportation the Tie that Binds), www.dot.gov

U.S. Agency for International Development, United States-Africa Partnership Revisited, www.usaid.gov/regions/afr/us-africa

"The President's Initiatives: Building the U.S.-Africa Partnership Hand-in-Hand in the 21st Century," The Government Printing Office, ISBN-X7229122

U.S. Embassy, Egypt, U.S.-Egypt Partnership for Economic Growth and Development, Fact Sheet and Current Activities, www.usembassy.egnet.net/usegypt/facts.html

Strengthening Human and Infrastructure Development

The White House, www.whitehouse.gov/africa
- Education in Africa
- Children's Initiatives
- Health and Family Planning in Africa
- Executive Order 13155, Access to HIV/AIDs Pharmaceuticals and Medical Technologies

U.S. House of Representatives, Committee on International Relations, Subcommittee on Africa, Statement by Calvin Humphrey on March 16, 2000

U.S. Agency for International Development
- Office of Sustainable Development, Bureau for Africa, "Education for Development and Democracy Initiative—An Interagency Strategy"
- USAID Progress on the President's Africa Initiatives, www.usaid.gov

U.S. Department of State
- Office of the Spokesman, Press Statement, African Women Entrepreneurs Expand Knowledge of Economic Empowerment, September 19, 2000
- Office of the Senior Coordinator for International Women's Issues, Female Genital Mutilation/Female Genital Cutting, September 9, 1999

"The President's Initiatives: Building the U.S.-Africa Partnership Hand-in-Hand in the 21st Century," The Government Printing Office, ISBN-X7229122

Index

The President departs a press conference with Nelson Mandela.

Don't judge a man at his worst,

judge him at his best.

By Reverend Victoria Ogun

Photo Credit: Shawn Farmer / The White House